"It is rare that you find honesty and humility as well as honor in modern leaders. However, Ray Ortlund has exhibited such qualities and earned respect across multiple arenas. When a potential vacancy arose for the chaplaincy in the United States Congress, Ray Ortlund was first on our list. It is this level of trustworthiness that allows Ray to challenge the stronghold of exploitation endemic to pornography. Ray's transparent approach cuts through the superficial layers, getting to the heart of the matter. This is a book that everyone should read, reminding us all of the value of being created in God's image."

Mark Walker, former congressman, North Carolina

"The subject of pornography tends to be embarrassing and can evoke feelings of helplessness and shame. Ray Ortlund refuses to pile onto that shame, and he wants you to know you're not helpless. Like a loving and compassionate father, he calls us to freedom, to a better life, and to the death of porn's grip on our imaginations that robs us of the true and beautiful intimacy our souls desperately hunger for."

Matt Chandler, Lead Pastor, The Village Church, Dallas, Texas; President, Acts 29 Church Planting Network; author, *The Mingling of Souls* and *The Explicit Gospel*

"In the pages of this book, Ray beautifully and compellingly calls us to be men of integrity building a world of nobility. He does this winsomely, graciously, and wisely in the form of letters infused with the tenderness and manliness of a father to his dear sons. I truly believe this book has the potential to be a culture changer. It will certainly impact, for the better, all who read and heed its wise and noble call."

Brian Brodersen, Pastor, Calvary Chapel, Costa Mesa, California

"Over the last couple years, I've gotten to know Ray Ortlund on a deeper level. He's struck me as a man of integrity and conviction, so when I heard he was writing a book to help Christians fight this evil thing called porn, I wasn't surprised. His book is a great blend of theological depth and relatable, practical tools that I believe will help all people battle pornography use and addiction. Porn destroys families, relationships, and marriages, but most of all, it keeps us distant from God and near our shame. Thank you, Ray, for tackling this topic with such boldness and truth. Heaven is smiling at you."

Preston Perry, poet; performance artist; teacher; apologist

"*The Death of Porn* is the kind of book I want my sons and daughters to read. With sage counsel, Ray Ortlund tenderly leads and courageously calls us to envision a world free from the plague of pornography. This book inspires contrition over sin, instills courage against sin, and compels us to cast our hope fully upon Jesus."

Garrett Kell, Pastor, Del Ray Baptist Church, Alexandria, Virginia; author, *Pure in Heart: Sexual Sin and the Promises of God*

"*The Death of Porn* is a magnificent work of hope. Ray Ortlund does not shame us or flatter us. He lifts us into a sense of our own destiny—not with his words but with God's. This book deepened my resolve to avoid living beneath my God-given dignity and to carve out a world of nobility as never before. We allowed porn in. By God's grace, we can drive it out. It's what we were born to do. If I could, I would put this book into the hands of every man in my generation."

T. J. Tims, Lead Pastor, Immanuel Church, Nashville, Tennessee

The Death of Porn

Dear friend,
    My heart longs to
reach your heart
through these letters.
Thank you for your
openness.
                —Ray

The Death of Porn

Men of Integrity Building a World of Nobility

Ray Ortlund

Foreword by Thabiti Anyabwile

:: CROSSWAY®

WHEATON, ILLINOIS

Published by Crossway
          1300 Crescent Street
          Wheaton, Illinois 60187

Published in association with the literary agency of Wolgemuth & Associates.

Cover design: Brian Bobel

First printing 2021

Printed in the United States of America

Trade paperback ISBN: 978-1-4335-7669-0
Epub ISBN: 978-1-4335-7672-0
PDF ISBN: 978-1-4335-7670-6
Mobipocket ISBN: 978-1-4335-7671-3

Library of Congress Cataloging-in-Publication Data

Names: Ortlund, Raymond C., Jr. author.
Title: The death of porn : men of integrity building a world of nobility / Ray Ortlund ; foreword by Thabiti Anyabwile.
Description: Wheaton, Illinois : Crossway, 2021. | Includes bibliographical references and index.
Identifiers: LCCN 2021002537 (print) | LCCN 2021002538 (ebook) | ISBN 9781433576690 (trade paperback) | ISBN 9781433576706 (pdf) | ISBN 9781433576713 (mobipocket) | ISBN 9781433576720 (epub)
Subjects: LCSH: Pornography—Religious aspects—Christianity. | Christian men—Sexual behavior. | Christian men—Conduct of life.
Classification: LCC BV4597.6 .O78 2021 (print) | LCC BV4597.6 (ebook) | DDC 241/.667—dc23
LC record available at https://lccn.loc.gov/2021002537
LC ebook record available at https://lccn.loc.gov/2021002538

Crossway is a publishing ministry of Good News Publishers.

LSC		30	29	28	27	26	25	24	23	22	21
15	14	13	12	11	10	9	8	7	6	5	4	3	2	1

For my grandsons—
may you thrive as men of integrity.

And for my granddaughters—
may you flourish in a world of nobility.

Contents

Foreword

EVEN TO SOME OF US OLDER CATS, Ray Ortlund is a father figure. He gained that status not through assertion, position, or power but through encouragement, exhortation, empathy, and a seemingly boundless energy for Jesus. He's the kind of man you admire because you have the unshakeable sense that he loves you. And not just you. Everybody.

This is why Ray is an ideal choice for addressing one of the biggest scourges of our time—pornography. Right now, in homes, offices, and cars across the country, pornography is attaching its tentacles to the eyes, minds, and hearts of men, women, boys, and girls. It's sneaking into the lives of innocents through click bait and thirst traps. Pornography is attempting to tighten its grip on teenagers exploding with pubescent change, married men and women courting wanderlust in joyless as well as joyful marriages, and Christian leaders trying to maintain double lives of outward success and inward corruption. What used to be confined to magazines has made its way into the mainstream of society and the church.

Ray Ortlund understands that defeating the porn monster will not come by white-knuckle, jaw-clenched grit individually willing its way to victory when all other soldiers have fallen. Victory can be had, but only in the loving community of the local church with saints covenanted together to stand against the wiles of the enemy in the truth of Jesus's gospel and the power of the Holy Spirit.

Ray understands that a teammate's hug is a much stronger weapon than a fan's pat on the back with a "dat a boy." That's why he writes about this most sensitive and dangerous subject with the tone and warmth of a fellow traveler.

In this book, Ray uses words to God-glorifying, soul-edifying effect. It's not that he's being clever or flattering. His words are simply devastating—in a good way. It's the effect of his sincerity! If out of the abundance of the heart the mouth speaks, then deep in the wells of Ray's heart is a reservoir of fragrant balm and strengthening sweetness. Not the off-the-shelf sweetness of sugary snacks cheapened by additives and preservatives. These pages give us the mature sweetness of aging, like fine maple syrup, tapped with humility and experience, oozing from his heart to the reader's.

As you read this book, you get the sense that this is what the apostle Paul meant when describing his ministry among the Thessalonians:

> But we were gentle among you, like a nursing mother taking care of her own children. . . .
>
> For you know how, like a father with his children, we exhorted each one of you and encouraged you and charged you to walk in a manner worthy of God, who calls you into his own kingdom and glory. (1 Thess. 2:7, 11–12)

I don't know what kind of book on pornography you expected to read. But I suspect this book will surprise you with that strength of Christ that comes from love. It will remind you of who you are in Christ, of who the men and women around you are in God's image, of the fact that you are not alone. There is help. There is victory.

There is a way to regain the regality of being royalty, because God in Christ is renewing you and me in his image.

This book speaks to the discouraged and distracted, the suffering and sullen, the unbelieving and the unsuspecting, the haughty and the halting. It's for everyone who, even for a moment, thinks victory over pornography is not possible. It's for you because victory is not only possible—victory has been accomplished for us by Jesus the risen Savior.

Come, let Ray introduce you to this Jesus and shepherd you to the freedom and joy found in him.

Thabiti Anyabwile
Pastor, Anacostia River Church
Washington, DC

Introduction

The Backstory

THANKS FOR PICKING UP THIS BOOK. I hope it helps. I hope it changes things. A lot of things.

I hope reading it messes with you. Writing it sure has messed with me.

Here's all you need to know about me:

- I am a Christian pastor.
- I love my wife.
- I am not looking at porn.
- I am a sexual sinner.

I wish that last one weren't true. But there's a brothel in the neighborhood of my mind, and I've wandered in there a time or two. It's a big part of why I'm thankful for the grace of Jesus. Never once has a stop-off at that Fantasyland made my life better. And never once has Jesus refused to take me back and clean me up.

If you're a sexual sinner too, this book is for you. Not the outwardly okay you, but the inwardly messy you. The real you, like the real me.

This book is *not* about you just getting polished up a bit here and there, making yourself more socially presentable. It's about your heart finally daring to believe in your true royalty. It's about the "real you" gaining traction for new integrity, especially in honest brotherhood with other men. It's about you, with other magnificent young men like you, building a new world of nobility, where both men *and* women can flourish.

What got me started on this book was a letter written over two hundred years ago. In the final days of his life, John Wesley, a minister in the Church of England, wrote a letter to a young politician named William Wilberforce. Wesley had urged him to use his political clout for opposing the slave trade in the British Empire. Wilberforce did. He made that fight his life mission. He was bitterly opposed by powerful people. But with God's help, Wilberforce and his allies finally defeated the slave trade and made the world a better place.

Here is Wesley's letter. And please overlook the old-fashioned style! Just notice what Wesley was asking Wilberforce to do— to take a bold stand against a successful evil that many people accepted as no big deal.

Dear Sir,

Unless the divine power has raised you up to be as Athanasius *contra mundum*,[1] I see not how you can go through your glorious enterprise in opposing that execrable villainy which is the scandal of religion, of England, and of human nature. Unless God has raised you up for this very thing, you will be worn out by the

---

1 Athanasius was a fourth-century bishop of Alexandria, in Egypt. He opposed the widespread heresy known as Arianism. He was so outnumbered, he became known as "Athanasius against the world."

opposition of men and devils. But if God be for you, who can be against you? Are all of them together stronger than God? O be not weary of well doing! Go on, in the name of God and in the power of His might, till even American slavery (the vilest that ever saw the sun) shall vanish away before it.

Reading this morning a tract written by a poor African,[2] I was particularly struck by that circumstance that a man who has black skin, being wronged or outraged by a white man, can have no redress, it being a law in all our colonies that the oath of a black against a white goes for nothing. What villainy is this!

That He who has guided you from youth up may continue to strengthen you in this and all things is the prayer of,

Dear Sir,
Your affectionate servant,
John Wesley

BALAM

24 FEB. 1791[3]

I love that. The dignified "Dear Sir," the inspiring "glorious enterprise," the blunt "execrable[4] villainy," the realistic "opposition of men and devils." Sign me up!

Anyway, this old letter got me thinking: *What about us today? What if not just one man but a whole generation of men takes a bold stand against the new slave trade of our time—pornography?* Slavery

---

2 Wesley is referring to Gustavus Vassa, born in Africa in 1745, kidnapped and sold as a slave in Barbados, and brought to England in 1757.

3 Spelling, capitalization, and punctuation adapted from the digitized manuscript of Wesley's letter, Methodist Library at Drew University, December 6, 2005, http://methodistlibrary .blogspot.com/2005/12/as-promised-more-digital-wesley.html.

4 "Execrable" means "deserving damnation."

is not gone. It's still going strong, but in a new form. Multitudes of men and women are in bondage to the degrading slavery of porn.

Which makes porn a *justice* issue. And Son, I know you're not okay with injustice! You know how God's heart breaks when people are oppressed and vandalized and dehumanized. But did you know he's calling you—just as he called Wilberforce—to do something about it? And you *can* do something about it, because God himself will help you.

Yes, the human odds are against you. The porn industry has dug in. It won't loosen its grip easily. Many people in our day just accept it—the way people accepted racialized slavery back then. That's why Wesley mentioned "Athanasius against the world." Athanasius was a heroic man who went up against impossible odds, confronting a major wrong in his time for the sake of future generations. And he won, because God was with him—the way God is with you today.

Yes, *you*. Almighty God above is *with* you.

Don't tell yourself you're into your own sexual sin too deep to get free, much less to set others free. You have a future worth reaching for. I want to help you get there.

Here's what I ask you to remember all along the way. Your battle against porn isn't about porn. It isn't about sex. It isn't about will-power. Your battle is about hope. It's about your heart believing that in spite of your many sins—like my many sins—God *rejoices* to give you a future you can scarcely dream of. You'll win your fight by believing that *God's love for you is too great to be limited to what you deserve.*

If you see yourself living under a grim law of crime and punishment, with you always getting the karma you deserve, your hope will die. Your despair will sink you down into resignation, and from there you'll spiral down into porn and shame, then more porn and more shame, and on and on. You know what I mean.

But I'm asking you to *defy* all despair, because God gives his best to men who deserve his worst. I'm asking you to believe the Bible: "But God shows his love for us in that *while we were still sinners*, Christ died for us" (Rom. 5:8). I'm asking you to reject the hell your sins deserve. I'm asking you to sin against your sins. I'm asking you to receive, with the empty hands of faith, a future so magnificent it can only come from the grace of God. When your heart grabs on to that hope, porn's spell is broken, and your freedom is dawning. So maybe you *are* a mess. But with Jesus, you're a messy *winner*, because you're *his* mess. And so am I.

Let's start this journey together by you and me choosing to flat-out *believe* the most repeated verse in the Bible—that our Lord is "a God merciful and gracious, slow to anger, and abounding in steadfast love and faithfulness" (Ex. 34:6). His personality profile is not balanced but biased—in favor of grace for the undeserving.[5]

Everything I'm going to say flows from this bright certainty about who God *really* is.

And once you've settled in your mind that you do have a future worth getting excited about, then you can help form a rebel movement—defiant young men who will someday dance on porn's grave, multitudes of men no longer groveling but standing tall and loving life again. And all of it, thanks to God.

That old letter from John Wesley is why I've written each chapter here as a letter—from me to you, from an older man to a younger man, calling you to give your life to this sacred cause of liberation. But it isn't just me. *God* is calling you to grow a counterculture where countless men and women can get their lives back, better than before, and forever.

---

5 Sam Allberry, "The Most Repeated Verse in the Bible," Desiring God (website), October 3, 2018, https://www.desiringgod.org/articles/the-most-repeated-verse-in-the-bible.

That's why I wrote this book—to start a movement. Because you matter, and everyone matters. And when *God* gets involved, we stop limiting how much good we can receive from him and how much good we can give to the world.

I don't expect to live many more years. But if this book helps you bring some healing to our injured world, I'll come to my dying day a happier man.

PART 1

REINTRODUCING
THE CHARACTERS

1

You Are Royalty

DEAR SON,

You matter. You matter more than you know. That's what I want to talk to you about—your dignity before God, what it's worth to you, and how it empowers you to change the future.

Do you believe in your own nobility? Yes, you're a nice guy. But being a nice, likeable guy hardly rises to the stature of your true destiny.

Long ago a Christian leader named Irenaeus got right to the point: "The glory of God is a man fully alive."[1] I believe that. I believe it about *you*. And what I'm saying is this: I see a new you not far off in the distant future—a you with sparkle in your eye and spring in your step and steel in your spine, a you more fully alive than you've ever been before. And the more this new you shows up now, the more alive the whole world will be.

Can we think that through together?

---

[1] This is a paraphrase of Irenaeus's literal wording "The glory of God is a living man." See *Five Books of S. Irenaeus: Against Heresies*, trans. John Keble (London, 1872), 369.

First off, I *have* to say this: I want you to become a better man than I've been.

I still remember a painful moment from over fifty years ago. I was doing some modeling in Hollywood. Suntan lotion advertisements. Teenagers in swimsuits. (Go ahead and laugh!) But a girl was in the photo shoot with me. She was sweet and kind.

During a break in our workday there at the studio, I wandered into the room where the makeup guy was set up. There was the girl, standing on a chair, with him in front of her, daubing some makeup on her body. Her face was turned aside, burning with shame. Instead of her swimsuit top, she had a scarf stretched across her breasts, one end under each arm, barely covering her. The predatory makeup guy had somehow gotten her top off, and she was trying to cover up as much as she could. But he had taken power over her. He had violated her dignity. And she had to stand there, with him right in front of her, touching her over and over with his makeup brush—and maybe with more. I get angry every time I think about it.

But at that moment, as I walked in and the scene broke upon me in an instant, I was shocked. I had never imagined such evil. I had no idea what to do. So I did nothing.

I turned around and walked out.

My thought was *I'll minimize this embarrassment.* I didn't want to make a bad situation even worse. But I should have stood up for her!

To my dying day, I will regret that moment. When that girl needed help against the bad guy, I let her down. Not because I despised her. Not at all. I was just oblivious. I had *zero* awareness of the actual grandeur of *my* royalty and *her* royalty. It had never dawned on me that God himself was leading me into every moment to help more people experience their true grandeur. I didn't know to wake up every morning mentally prepared to bring God's kingdom of royalty into whatever the day might reveal—like protecting a girl over in Hollywood who was getting pushed around.

I was an immature, fun-loving guy with a problem. My life was about me—not her. Where's the nobility in that?

What I now know is this. I am a knight in service to the King of kings here in a brutal world. The age-old ideals of chivalry—courage, justice, loyalty, courtesy toward women[2]—my King lived and died that way. I'm learning how to live his way. Can we learn together? If you embrace your high calling earlier in life than I did, you'll do so much good. You'll be ready for anything. Even at a moment's notice. Especially at a moment's notice.

So let's think about who you really are.

Well, before that, let's settle the question of who you *aren't*. This world has no idea what you're really worth. Around here you are, at best, useful. You fit into a market niche or a voting bloc or some other impersonal category, to be manipulated for someone's selfish agenda.

But that is *not* who you are.

———

The truth is, you are *royalty*.

———

Britain has its royal family, with the pomp and ceremony. I respect that. But you belong to a royal family from beyond all this world. So how crazy is it that you might feel like God is up there rolling his eyes at you, thinking what an idiot you are! The God who is actually out there respects you. To him you're not a pawn, not a loser. In God's eyes, you have royal dignity.

2   O. B. Duane, *The Origins of Wisdom: Chivalry* (London: Brockhampton, 1997), 86 et passim.

Here's why I'm so sure about it. The Bible says that, long before target marketing and voting blocs and all the rest of it, your story began here:

God created man in his own image,
> in the image of God he created him;
> > male and female he created them. (Gen. 1:27)

You didn't pop into existence by mere chance. You didn't bubble up from the primordial goo. You were created by the King of the universe. Which means you have stature here in his world.

The heavens are the LORD's heavens,
> but the earth he has given to the children of man. (Ps. 115:16)

As a God-created man, you have every right to see yourself as "crowned with glory and honor" (Ps. 8:5). You don't have to *make* this true. It *is* true. Your creation was your coronation.

The Hebrew word translated "image" in Genesis 1:27 is used elsewhere in the Bible to mean a statue.[3] You aren't a literal statue of God. He has no form, no edges, no limits. But you do "image" God as you think like him and love like him and stand up for him. You can think of it this way: "Just as powerful earthly kings, to indicate their claim to dominion, erect an image of themselves in the provinces of their empire where they do not personally appear, so man is placed upon earth in God's image as God's sovereign emblem."[4]

Your identity—who you really are—is found in the King you represent. You are his royal ambassador to our broken world.

---

3 For example, Amos 5:26.
4 Gerhard von Rad, *Genesis: A Commentary*, trans. John H. Marks (Philadelphia: Westminster, 1961), 60.

Do you see now why I believe your life counts for so much? God sure isn't asking you to settle for mediocrity. He designed you to reach for nothing less than your own personal grandeur, for the display of his glory.

Way down deep, you know this. When you were a kid and someone asked you, "What do you want to be when you grow up?" you never said, "When I grow up, I'm gonna be *wishy-washy!*" No way. You said, "I want to be a fighter pilot" or "I want to be a Navy SEAL" or something else big and bold. Even in your boyhood, your God-created nobility was already longing to be fulfilled. God himself put into your heart a sense of destiny.

So, what's happened to that? How did a man created for greatness become disappointed with his life? Why does a man—a man like you, with your God-given stature—ever feel bogged down and held back?

Let me tell you one thing, in case your mind goes here first. It's not because you aren't religious enough.

Religion says, "Do better, try harder, pedal faster." Religion says you've got work to do if you ever hope to get back on God's good side. But that's not what God says. The defeatist message of religion, shaming you as a failure, is not God talking to you. It's your own guilty conscience pretending to be God. And no one is helped by being scolded.

What does help? When your heavenly Father breaks through the noise of who you *aren't*—the cheap lies in your mind, the exhausting clutter in your life—and he speaks his truth to you. And you start believing him. You start accepting your mission to "image" his glory in your generation.

And that's how you start getting traction for a new you—when you dare to believe that God your King created you for a purpose of greatness.

Think of the glory of your manhood—the capacity of your mind, the range of your emotions, the potential of your career, the beauty of your relationships, the mystery of your sexuality. And God wants to squeeze all that amazingness down into a tiny prison cell of boring religiosity? That's the God-denying craziness that destroys the future you want before it's even had a chance.

Here is the truth about you, Son. Your foundational, God-created self—the *you* that you are—is not a problem you're stuck with. Not at all.

———

Your God-created you is a strategy he wants to unleash.

———

Your human totality is a *gift* from your Father. You are a brilliantly created and fully equipped man, just right for your mission here in his world. Long ago, God formed a plan to bring evil down and to lift freedom up. *You* are part of God's plan. Why not give yourself permission to believe it?

If you still suspect I'm trying to recruit you for more religion, I don't blame you. We pastors can be hypocritical. That's on me. But your problem is *not* that you haven't obsessed enough about how religious you should be. Your problem is that you haven't stared transfixed at the grandeur of God's lofty purpose for you.

You drift along in your nice-guy blah whatever. You experience some highs and lows along the way. Maybe even more highs than lows. But how on earth can some above-average existence possibly satisfy you? The you on whom *God* has put a noble calling!

It's not as though you've failed to live your dream. It's that your dream is too small. That's why sometimes you hate your life, why you feel angry and moody and frustrated. Not royal. Not fully alive.

Your ideal dream life is like air. When a guy is hungry, it doesn't matter how much air he inhales. Air *cannot* satisfy hunger. When you settle for less than your true dignity, you're like a starving man in a world of air. Your hunger will never stop gnawing at you as long as you keep gulping down the airy nothings of this world's fraudulent categories.

How could it be otherwise? If you trivialize God, you inevitably trivialize your God-created self. Don't hold at arm's length the very One who understands you better than you understand yourself. You risk losing your one chance at life.

It's your lack of God that explains your lack of grandeur.

How else can you explain why you, created for mastery, grind out the treadmill of your job? Or why you, created for dignity, grovel before degrading porn sites? Or why you, created for destiny, settle for mere popularity? Or why you, created for authority, can't control your own moods?

Jesus got right to the point: "Everyone who sins is a slave of sin" (John 8:34 NLT). We know sin is bad. But Jesus helps us admit where sin takes us—slavery. We men, born to be kings, aren't even in command of ourselves.

In the classic film *Lawrence of Arabia,* Lawrence finally has an honest conversation with his friend Ali about what he's really facing deep inside:

LAWRENCE: I've come to the end of myself. . . .

ALI: "A man can be whatever he wants." You said.

LAWRENCE: I'm sorry. I thought it was true.

ALI: You proved it!

LAWRENCE [opening his shirt and grabbing the flesh of his chest]: Look, Ali, look. *That's* me! . . . And there's nothing I can *do* about it.

ALI: "A man can *do* whatever he wants." You said.

LAWRENCE: He can. But—he can't *want* what he wants. [He touches his chest again.] *This* is the stuff that decides what he wants.[5]

We're told in our world today that we can succeed by making good choices based on good information. Really? It's that easy? Sometimes we tell ourselves we can sneak up close to the line between right and wrong and play there a while without actually crossing the line. And we can easily turn back before we go too far or get caught. But hasn't our own experience proven this a lie? Again and again?

The truth is, sin is as unchosen as hunger, as comfortable as sleep, as inevitable as gravity, as lethal as poison. Sin offers itself as an option, but it takes over as a master. How can we rise to our true royalty when our deeper impulses keep dragging us down as slaves to resignation, exhaustion, apathy?

The next time you hear a college graduation speaker tell everyone they can be and do whatever they put their minds to—if that were true, we'd have found our way by now, don't you think?[6] The real reason we keep falling on our faces is so serious that it demands plain language. You and I have a problem: *evil*.

Man, I hate that. But it's real. We're not good men who mess up now and then. We are bad men who prove it every day. What's more, this grim assessment is equally true of everyone: "For *all* have sinned and fall short of the glory of God" (Rom. 3:23). We're all

---

5 Robert Bolt, *Lawrence of Arabia*, http://www.dailyscript.com/scripts/Lawerence_of_Arabia .pdf, part 2, scene 163.

6 David Brooks, *The Second Mountain: The Quest for a Moral Life* (New York: Random House, 2019), 14: "We hand [these speeches] over like some great, awesome presents. And it turns out these presents are great big boxes of nothing."

like Jason Bourne. We're trying to figure out who we are. But the more we discover, the less we like what we find.

Think of it this way. If evil were the color yellow, like police tape at a crime scene, then everything about us, all the time, at all levels, would show some shade of yellow. Even our "good moments" glow yellowish—far from the radiance God created us for.

The brilliant author G. K. Chesterton was asked the mega-question "What's wrong with the world?" His answer? "I am."[7] We all need it that blunt. Then we can stop believing in our own quick fixes.

Like when we say to God: "Okay, Lord, I'm going to change. And this time I really mean it. I'm going to *prove* to you how serious I am." And we do try. But we can't make it stick. Pretty soon we're back in the same old mess. Why? Because we're a complicated mix of two opposites:

We are *royal*, and we are *evil*.

Yes, it's that dire. That's what we're up against—a battle raging right inside us. But still, God's whole heart is *for us*. I love how Dietrich Bonhoeffer put it:

> You are a sinner, a great, desperate sinner; now come, as the sinner that you are, to God who loves you. He wants you as you are; He does not want anything from you, a sacrifice, a work; He wants you alone.

---

7 "What's Wrong with the World?," The Apostolate of Common Sense, April 29, 2012, https://www.chesterton.org/wrong-with-world/.

You can hide nothing from God. The mask you wear before men will do you no good before Him. He wants to see you as you are, He wants to be gracious to you. You do not have to go on lying to yourself and your brothers, as if you were without sin; you can dare to be a sinner.[8]

What use is some patching up here and there, with better polish and manners, when evil lives within us like a dirty squatter in a once-grand palace? But you can "dare to be a sinner," because God can re-create you in his image all over again.

Here's how we face our extreme need: by realizing God himself has already faced it.

An African child asked her mother, "What is God doing all day long?" Her mom's wise answer was "He spends his whole day mending broken things."[9] What else does he have to work with? He specializes in turning hopeless cases into stunning successes. But not through any religious do-better-try-harder. God does it through Jesus, who now comes into the picture, center-stage.

———

Jesus renews our royalty.

———

When everything was on the line for us, with our dignity hopelessly damaged by our recklessness, God simply changed the subject. He changed it from us and our shame to Jesus and his grace. Not Jesus as an inspiring example we should imitate but Jesus as the better self we've never been. Our King lived for us the royal

8   Dietrich Bonhoeffer, *Life Together* (New York: Harper, 1954), 111.
9   Richard H. Schmidt, *Glorious Companions: Five Centuries of Anglican Spirituality* (Grand Rapids, MI: Eerdmans, 2002), 320.

life we should have lived and died for us the shameful death we should have died.

This magnificent man—"the image of the invisible God" (Col. 1:15), the "exact imprint" of God's nature (Heb. 1:3)—we didn't welcome him into our world on a red carpet. We blamed him for our misery and humiliated him at the cross.

The whole point of crucifixion was not just to kill a man but to demean him while killing him. Never more than in Jesus's death. The nakedness, the mocking, the spitting, with the crown of thorns and the purple robe—it was the humiliating "inversion of his kingship."[10] The cross was like a lynching in the Old South—white rage vented on a scapegoat.[11] Jesus understands shame.

But the cross was more. Amazingly, the cross was where God started bending our evil around to restore us. We thought we were getting rid of Jesus, but God made sure we'd get ourselves back. At the cross, we proved how bad we are to God, but God proved how good he is to us. In C. S. Lewis's story *The Magician's Nephew*, Aslan the lion—the Christ figure—makes this promise about our evil: "I will see to it that the worst falls upon myself."[12]

At the cross, God didn't sweep our evil under the rug but exposed it and paid for it. The love of God is not a cheap compromise. His forgiveness is noble forgiveness. That's why when *God* washes you clean of all your sins in the blood of Christ, you can allow yourself to *feel* forgiven. Feeling new is the *right* response to the cross. Freedom is what God *wants* for you. The cross was the price he was willing to pay. You can accept his grace with a clear conscience.

---

10 Fleming Rutledge, *The Crucifixion: Understanding the Death of Jesus Christ* (Grand Rapids, MI: Eerdmans, 2015), 96.

11 William Edgar, "Justification and Violence," in *Justified in Christ: God's Plan for Us in Justification*, ed. K. Scott Oliphant (Fearn: Mentor, 2007), 132–36.

12 C. S. Lewis, *The Magician's Nephew* (New York: Collier, 1972), 136.

Maybe you look at your mess and think: *If God has any self-respect at all, he must despise me. He'd be wrong* not *to despise me.* But that despairing thought keeps you hanging back from God. Self-punishment doesn't make you more forgivable. It blocks your way to forgiveness. He is *inviting* you to come out of hiding and stand tall again. He's not at war with you. Why? Because you aren't really all that bad? No. Because in one blinding moment of painful atonement on the cross, the dark energy of your evil forever lost its bid for supremacy.

Do you really think, after the cross, your shame drives God away? Nope. Your shame is precisely where he can re-create you the most gloriously. You think you're disgusting to him? Wrong again. The worst things about you are where he loves you the most tenderly. God *welcomes* high-maintenance men who keep coming back to him for more mercy and more mercy and more mercy, multiple times every day. He isn't tired, and he isn't tired of *you.*

He proved his commitment long ago. At the cross.

So now you know why you can have your glory back. Not because you have what it takes, but because he does. Not because you haven't damaged yourself that badly, but because Jesus restores your dignity that decisively, "bringing many sons to glory" (Heb. 2:10). Your evil cannot have the final say over you once you've handed it over to him.

He is why I have such high hopes for you—and for other guys like you.

He's not angry, not sulking, not holding out. He's got skin in this game—literally. He is personally invested in seeing you flourishing in your full royalty again.

When you come to Jesus for the forgiveness you don't deserve and the re-creation you can't cause, how does he respond? He is downright happy to give you his royal best. Don't worry that he might change his mind later if you screw up again—and then again. The actual Jesus you're dealing with knows only one way to love—*his* way. Which means not just grace but "grace upon grace" (John 1:16)—endless grace. It is his exuberant love for you, not your feeble love for him, that will lift you all the way to your eternal crown (1 Cor. 15:49).

Bottom line: "If anyone is in Christ, he is *a new creation*. The old has passed away; behold, the new has come" (2 Cor. 5:17).

Son, come back to your royalty.

Here's why you can: "He sides with you against your sin, not against you because of your sin."[13] Don't try to figure that out. His big heart makes no sense to our puny brains. But here's the great thing about hitting rock bottom. All we can do then is receive his grace.

Your true royalty as your certain destiny—why not sign up? All you stand to lose is what you hate about your life anyway. So here is a simple prayer *any* man can pray: "Lord Jesus, I need nothing less than a new me. Please? I'm open now."

Well, that's enough for one letter. I'll close by asking you to take two decisive steps right now.

One, accept that Jesus considers you worth fighting for. You don't have to clean yourself up first. He'll reinstate you as his warrior for his kingdom because of who *he* is. I love how this Lutheran pastor said it:

---

13 Dane Ortlund, *Gentle and Lowly: The Heart of Christ for Sinners and Sufferers* (Wheaton, IL: Crossway, 2020), 71.

We are justified freely, for Christ's sake, by faith, without the exertion of our own strength, gaining of merit, or doing of works. To the age-old question, "What shall I do to be saved?" the [Christian] answer is shocking: "Nothing! Just be still. Shut up and listen for once in your life to what God the Almighty, Creator and Redeemer, is saying to his world and to you in the death and resurrection of his Son! Listen and believe!"[14]

Two, prepare for battle. As a newly re-created image of the King, you will hear his call to take a stand in many battles in your generation. And here is one cause that *really* matters to him, and it *really* matters to you from your own experience: the evil oppression of porn. Your King is calling you not only to stop looking at porn but also to start pushing back against the industry that creates it. He is calling you to stand up as a liberated man liberating others.

My other letters will explain further what you, and other men with you, can do to serve his cause of "proclaim[ing] liberty to the captives" (Isa. 61:1).

Maybe you remember this scene from the film *Braveheart*. William Wallace, on horseback, has just called his ragtag band of Scottish troops to fight for their freedom. The massive English army is on the opposite side of the field. Wallace is with two friends, out in front of his army. The dialogue goes like this:

IRISH FRIEND: Fine speech. Now what do we do?
WALLACE: Just be yourselves. (*Turns to leave.*)
SCOTTISH FRIEND: Where you goin'?

---

14 Gerhard O. Forde, *Justification by Faith: A Matter of Death and Life* (Philadelphia: Fortress, 1982), 22.

WALLACE: I'm going to pick a fight. (*Rides off to the enemy.*)
SCOTTISH FRIEND: Well, we didn't get dressed up for nothin'.

You aren't getting "dressed up for nothin'" either. Jesus is picking a fight with the world of porn, and he's recruiting you to fight
alongside him. It will not be easy. But human dignity is a winning
cause, because he is in it. If I could somehow speak to your whole
generation, here's the question I'd ask:

Where are the young men of this generation who will hold their
lives cheap, and be faithful even unto death? Where are the ad-
venturers, the explorers, the buccaneers for God, who count one
human soul of far greater value than the rise or fall of an empire?
Where are God's men in this day of God's power?[15]

Because you matter,
Ray

---

15 Howard W. Guinness, *Sacrifice* (Chicago: InterVarsity Press, 1947), 59–60.

2

She Is Royalty

DEAR SON,

She matters too. She matters more than you know. That girl, that woman, the one on the porn site—she isn't just pixels on a screen. She's real. Somewhere, right now, she's out there trying to get by. I'll bet you any amount of money she didn't volunteer for porn. She was degraded and abused into it. And that precious woman has hopes and feelings and longings and sorrows, just like you. She is as human as you are, as worthy as you are, as royal as you are.

In this letter, I have some hard things to say. But here's where I'm going. I'm asking you to change how you see that woman on the porn site. I'm not asking you to make anything up. I'm only asking you to accept the way God sees her. He is on her side. He is indignant at the ways she is objectified, monetized, and mistreated.

Which leads me to ask you for something else. I'm also asking you to change how you treat her. I want you to stop abusing her and start defending her. You're doing one or the other. More on

39

that in a minute. But for now, just hold your emotional horses long enough to let me make my case.

The King of the universe created you to stand as royalty, advancing his kingdom. Let that awareness settle on you. Here's your next step: she is royalty too. God created *every* woman with high dignity and immeasurable worth. Whether or not any woman herself believes it, this is still true: God created her for majesty. *God* is why she matters. And no one has the right to degrade her, since God has dignified her. Whoever a woman is in his sight—that's what she's really worth.

Since, to God above, every woman is regal, cherished, worthy, it's about time we men demand of ourselves, and of all this world, that she be treated right.

Let's think back to that Scripture I quoted in my first letter. Remember the last line in that verse?

God created man in his own image;
in the image of God he created him;
male and female he created them. (Gen. 1:27)

Back when the Bible was written, nobody else was saying that. It's not as though human thought was evolving upward, inching its way toward the equal royalty of the sexes. It's not as though the ancient philosophers and gurus got the ball into the red zone, and then the Bible finally scored the touchdown. No, Genesis 1:27 surprised everyone. It was God speaking into our abusive world with a bold claim: a woman deserves all the respect any man deserves, because she is created in God's image as much as any man.

In the ancient world, people came up with their own versions of how we all got going. The Babylonians, for example, believed the human race was the brainstorm of the god Marduk:

Blood I will mass and cause bones to be.

I will establish a savage, "man" shall be his name.

Verily, savage-man I will create.[1]

The Babylonians saw themselves as savages, and they acted like it. Their creation story didn't even mention "male and female." But the Bible *celebrates* "male and female." Genesis 1:27 is the first poetry in all the Bible, because God rejoices over us men and women. He doesn't call us savage. He happily calls us royal—both man and woman equally.

But there's no woman like Eve in the Babylonian account of creation. The first woman in all of history, and not even an honorable mention! But the Bible? Adam's heart leaps with joyous love at first sight.

This at last is bone of my bones

and flesh of my flesh;

she shall be called Woman,

because she was taken out of Man. (Gen. 2:23)

These are the very first recorded human words, and again they are poetry. Adam welcomes Eve with relief: "This *at last.* . . ." He identifies with her, personally, closely, as "bone of my bones / and flesh of my flesh." He isn't threatened by her equality. It's the very thing that thrills him.

He just finished naming the animals there in the garden of Eden (Gen. 2:19–20). And lions and tigers have their place, I suppose. But only Eve has Adam's heart. She isn't property. She isn't a prize of

1 "The Creation Epic," trans. E. A. Speiser, in *Ancient Near Eastern Texts Relating to the Old Testament*, ed. James B. Pritchard (Princeton, NJ: Princeton University Press, 1969), 68.

war. She isn't even—not yet, anyway—the mother of his children. In and of herself, by God's design, she is worthy to be celebrated. And Adam *loves* it this way—and embraces her.

We call this amazing human arrangement "marriage." It's the only place where a man and woman should experience each other sexually. It's where sex becomes the win-win God wants it to be: "And the man and his wife were both naked and were not ashamed" (Gen. 2:25). There they are, Adam and Eve, married by God, together in the garden of Eden, naked and sexual and both completely happy. And in that place of permanent belonging and gentle acceptance, the woman isn't the only one naked and vulnerable. She isn't exploited, shared, or sold. They are *both* naked, and not ashamed or degraded or used, but comfortably at ease, fully accepted, tenderly embraced.[2]

A man and a woman can still experience this today, under the blessing of God, within marriage. Through their wedding vows, they give up their solo futures and commit fully to one another. On their wedding day, they step inside the circle of the "one flesh" union of marriage (Gen. 2:24), where they share everything.

Everything.

Other healthy relationships limit how far things will go. What's unique about marriage is the unlimited openness a man and a woman joyfully sign up for. It's why marriage is sealed, celebrated, and refreshed through sex. Marriage is all about total sharing, total belonging—like real sex. Inside the circle where only a husband and wife fully belong, they cultivate safety and honor, so that sex is unashamedly joyful for both of them equally. When the minister

---

2   This rhetorical device ("not ashamed") is called *antenantiosis*, which uses the negative "in order to express the positive in a very high degree," according to F. W. Bullinger, *Figures of Speech Used in the Bible* (Grand Rapids, MI: Baker, 1971), 160. For example, if I say, "He is no fool," I mean, "He is very wise." I thank Dr. Bruce Waltke for pointing this out to me.

concludes their wedding ceremony with "You may now kiss the bride," he is saying, "Let the sex, as God meant it to be, finally begin!" Are the man and woman still vulnerable? More than ever. But for that very reason, their intimacy is all the more wondrous.

Now let's fast-forward to the end of the Bible, where we finally see the point of it all. The risen Jesus will not merely upgrade this existence we're stuck with now. He will lift us into "a new heaven and a new earth," where we will "reign forever and ever" (Rev. 21:1; 22:5). In that sparkling new universe, every redeemed woman will stand in glory as a Queen of the New Creation. No matter how she has sinned in this world, no matter how she has been sinned against, she will be *radiantly royal forever and ever.*

In my mind's eye, I see her there even now. She stands like Lady Galadriel, queen of the elves in *The Lord of the Rings.* In Tolkien's vision, Galadriel is breathtaking with beauty, knowledge, and power. She speaks gravely, wisely, and courteously. She is mighty, fair, and fearless. When the Fellowship of the Ring must leave Lothlórien, Galadriel asks Gimli the dwarf what parting gift he would like to receive from her: "'None, Lady,' answered Gimli. 'It is enough for me to have seen the Lady of the Galadhrim, and to have heard her gentle words.'"

Galadriel is surprised by his humility. So she encourages him to go ahead and ask for something so that he isn't the only visitor to leave without a token of their solidarity:

> "There is nothing, Lady Galadriel," said Gimli, bowing low and stammering. "Nothing, unless it might be—unless it is permitted to ask, nay, to name a single strand of your hair, which surpasses the gold of the earth as the stars surpass the gems of the mine. I do not ask for such a gift. But you commanded me to name my desire."

The elves are astonished by his audacious request. But Galadriel smiles with approval:

> "None have ever made to me a request so bold and yet so courteous. And how shall I refuse, since I commanded him to speak? But tell me, what would you do with such a gift?"
>
> "Treasure it, Lady," he answered. ". . . And if ever I return to the smithies of my home, it shall be set in imperishable crystal to be an heirloom of my house and a pledge of good-will between the Mountain and the Wood until the end of days."
>
> Then the lady unbraided one of her long tresses, and cut off three golden hairs, and laid them in Gimli's hand.[3]

Our world today is blind to the glories of true manhood and true womanhood. But the Bible teaches us men to respect every woman as a potential Galadriel, whose glory can, by God's grace, leave us awestruck forever.

The porn industry sure doesn't teach us to see women that way. That vile world is oblivious to a woman's actual glory. But now we know, thanks to the Bible, that every woman was created for a destiny so magnificent that the story of it cannot be fully told in all the ages of time. God's heart for her, God's purpose for her, can only be revealed in the eternal new creation. All this world, even at its best, is too small for her, too unworthy of her. And every woman—however much she suffers in this world—if she entrusts her future to the care of the risen King, he will tell her true story in the next world forever.

What C. S. Lewis said of everyone is no less true of every woman:

---

3   J. R. R Tolkien, *The Lord of the Rings: The Fellowship of the Ring* (London: HarperCollins, 2005), 376.

It is a serious thing to live in a society of possible gods and goddesses, to remember that the dullest and most uninteresting person you talk to may one day be a creature which, if you saw it now, you would be strongly tempted to worship, or else a horror and a corruption such as you now meet, if at all, only in a nightmare. All day long we are, in some degree, helping each other to one or other of these destinations. It is in the light of these overwhelming possibilities, it is with the awe and the circumspection proper to them, that we should conduct all our dealings with one another, all friendships, all loves, all play, all politics. There are no *ordinary* people.[4]

By now, Son, I'm guessing that a new realization is breaking upon you that every woman's sexuality is a sacred gift of God. Remember how Jesus taught us? "You have heard that it was said, 'You shall not commit adultery.' But I say to you that everyone who looks at a woman with lustful intent has already committed adultery with her in his heart" (Matt. 5:27–28).

To Jesus, even if we aren't literally touching, still, we are really taking. And, Jesus tell us, it's a violation of the sacred.

My friend Sam Allberry helps us face the seriousness of our sexualized thoughts about any woman we're not married to:

Jesus is saying that her sexuality is precious and valuable, that she has a sexual integrity to her which matters and should be honored by everyone else. *He is saying that this sexual integrity is so precious that it must not be violated, even in the privacy of someone else's mind.* Even if she were never to find out about it,

---

4 C. S. Lewis, *The Weight of Glory and Other Addresses* (Grand Rapids, MI: Eerdmans, 1974), 14–15. Italics original.

she would have been greatly wronged by being thought about lustfully. . . . Jesus is showing us that our sexuality is far more precious than we might have realized, and that his teaching is actually a form of protection for it.[5]

Okay, now we're ready to understand what porn really is. Porn is Satan recruiting us to degrade a woman into the *opposite* of who she is—from royalty to slavery.

Satan *hates* women. It was a woman, remember, who brought Jesus into this world, dooming Satan's evil kingdom forever. Satan cannot get his hands on the risen Jesus, but he sure can torment women. And he does. Porn is Satan—yes, *Satan*—assaulting women, denying their glory, dragging them down, because they remind him every day of the true King he hates and fears.

I want to make this as real as I can. So let me tell you about a brave friend of mine. Her name is Tara.[6] She is real. Her story is true. With her permission, here are some things she courageously revealed during a recent conversation:

My first memory in life was when I was four years old, and I was being assaulted in a bathroom. By the time I was eighteen, I had been hurt by eight people on many occasions. I can't remember a time in my life when I wasn't hurting or being hurt.

When I was trafficked, it wasn't like a violent kidnapping. The man was nice to me. His line was, "You should do these things

---

5   Sam Allberry, *Why Does God Care Who I Sleep With?* (Epsom, Surrey: Good Book, 2020), 18. Italics original.
6   Tara is her real name. She told me she wants her real name used because she's a real person with a real identity. Too many times in the past her personhood and identity were taken from her.

for me, because I'm taking care of you." No one had ever cared for me. Why wouldn't I be grateful?

He had me work in the sex clubs he owned, where I was used. He filmed me without my knowledge. The very first time I wondered, *How can I get through this?* Somehow I did get through it. Then I saw the camera.

I didn't get angry about all this. Why would I? Those feelings would've required me to be human, and I wasn't human. I didn't think of myself as human and worthy of being treated well. No one ever saw me as having potential or value. No one ever saw me as a person at all.

Some things in my past are hard to remember, because I had to detach from my body, my mind and my heart just to survive. I didn't have the luxury of feeling. I didn't have the luxury of being human. Nobody ever asked me what I wanted to be when I grew up. I didn't know there were options. For me, there weren't any. So I had to go along with the trafficking. What choice did I have? Hope for a better life? Hope was just another luxury not afforded to me.

The very things about me that men wanted to look at—to me, they were horrible. I hated myself. I still hate myself. I still battle shame every day.

Years later, after my husband left me, a neighbor told me about Jesus. We talked for hours. I told her that Jesus wouldn't want anything to do with me. I was sure of that. How could he? Nobody ever wanted me, except for sex. I didn't deserve to have a life. I thought—calmly, matter-of-factly—that I'd get my kids through high school and then end my life. I would just be done. Why not? Some people are meant to live, and I wasn't one of them. But through prayer and an army of friends that God surrounded me with, I came to realize Jesus had never abandoned me. He was there with me all the time. He wept with me. He wept *for* me. He is now restoring me. My life now is as opposite as it could be from where I used to be. That past is not who I am. I am not defined by what was done to me by them; I am defined by what was done *for* me by Him.

Tara is discovering her true royalty in Christ. Not every woman has that advantage. But every woman should have it.

Some women never get out of that prison. I'm one of the lucky ones. I should be dead by now. I should be a statistic. But Jesus saved me.

Eventually, I got a job with a Christian ministry. My boss and his wife gave me a chance. I worked hard and learned and did well and got promoted. They were the first people to ever tell me I had value. My boss then joined a larger ministry with incredible leaders, and I went to this new job. We've worked together now for seven years. I've finally been able to get not only the counseling I needed but also the loving fellowship of people who believe so much in me. A family. Because of these wonderful servants of God, I finally have my freedom.

I'm also remarried now. My husband knows everything. And he treats me like I'm a priceless treasure. I keep wondering, *When is he going to realize I don't deserve his love?* But he tells me all the time, "I want to spend every day, for the rest of my life, showing you how much Jesus loves you." And he does. I had never before seen a man treat a woman like royalty. It's ridiculously amazing.

Sometimes, I admit, I want to run from him. Pain is familiar. I'm used to it. I know what to expect. To be loved and valued is wonderful, but still sometimes confusing.

I asked Tara, "What would you want to say to men who look at porn?" Here's her answer:

What if it was your sister? The women used in the sex industry don't just have a face and a body. They have a soul too. They have a name. No woman grows up thinking, *I hope I'll spend my life being abused.* But every woman in porn has been trafficked. Trafficking is simply making a profit from someone's sex act. That's *every* woman in porn. It's *all* coercive. Every woman is under duress. Every woman would rather be anywhere else.

If you want to know what it's really like, go sit in a dark closet for five minutes and see how it feels. Then imagine being kept in there for years and years.

For a guy, it's a short burst of sexual gratification, and then he moves on. But for the woman, the effects *from that single moment of sexual selfishness* can last for the rest of her life. Every moment of porn leaves behind a broken woman, sitting in the dark closet, raising her hand and saying, "But I'm still here. I'm a human being. I have feelings. I have a heart. I have a name."

Men must know we're real. And we don't want to hide any more. We want out of that closet.

I thank my heroic friend for pulling the curtain back, showing what's really going on behind the playful appearances.

Now let's face the truth. Online porn is a man siding with Satan. (Women look at porn too, but this is between you and me.) Porn is a man saying to that woman on the screen, that potential Galadriel: "I don't care about you. I don't care about your personal story that got you onto this wretched porn site. I don't care about what will happen to you when the filming is over—how you'll drag yourself back to your apartment and get drunk just to stop feeling the pain.

I don't care about what you'll be facing tomorrow, which will be yet another day of this torment. I don't *want* to know what you're suffering. I don't even want to know your name. *You* don't matter. All that matters here is *me*. And not the 'royal me' God created but the predatory me, the masturbatory me, the urge-of-the-moment me, the selfish me that Satan is robbing of life, even as I rob you of life. So whoever you are there on the screen—I'll click over to some other victim soon, but you just keep up the show, okay? Keep smiling while you're abused. Keep it up, while I masturbate and masturbate and masturbate, because *nothing about me or you really matters anyway.*"

The word for that evil mentality is *despair*. Dorothy Sayers calls it

the sin that believes in nothing, cares for nothing, seeks to know nothing, interferes with nothing, enjoys nothing, loves nothing, hates nothing, finds purpose in nothing, lives for nothing, and remains alive only because there is nothing it would die for. We have known it far too well for many years. The only thing perhaps we have not known about it is that it is a mortal sin.[7]

And a "mortal sin" is a sin so bad that, without repentance, it will damn us to eternal hell. The proof of that is how it turns this world into a living hell right now.

For example, a major porn site has been exposed for profiting from videos of rape, abuse, sadism, torture, racism, and trafficking uploaded by users. There is no accountability. No justice. No humanity. And when you go to such a site, do you realize what you're doing? You're walking into a big, semidarkened room, with

---

7 Dorothy L. Sayers, *Letters to a Diminished Church: Passionate Arguments for the Relevance of Christian Doctrine* (Nashville: W Publishing Group, 2004), 98.

lots of beds and couches and floor space. This room is crowded with sexual predators of many kinds, and the women and children in there are being tormented. The victims who look like they're having fun are faking it, because they'll be punished even more if they don't perform on command. And you're standing there at the doorway into that room looking around for the "decent" option for your enjoyment, because you're a good guy and not involved in the really bad stuff. *That's* where you are. *That's* what you're doing—when you *should* be turning up the lights and rescuing the victims and calling the police.

Every single girl in that horrible place matters to God above. If she doesn't matter to you too, then you've taken your stand not only against her, but even more, you've taken your stand with Satan against God.

But God, in mercy, is calling you to a complete turnaround. It starts with you becoming honest with yourself about where you're going and what you're supporting.

You'll start getting free when you start getting honest.

No man is helped by using nicey-nice hypocritical words like "I slipped up today." Or passive words like "This happened to me." Every man who wants his freedom back must start using true words that match what porn is. If you're watching it, you're doing it.

So how's this for next-level honesty? If you look at porn, be honest enough to say to God, "Today I entertained myself with sexual exploitation," or "Today I joined in the abuse of a woman," or "Today I watched her degradation for my pleasure," or "Today I took my stand against you and with Satan."

You think I'm going too far? No, I'm not. Again, look what Jesus said: "Everyone who looks at a woman with lustful intent has already committed adultery with her in his heart."

What is he saying? *The look is morally equivalent to the act.* Yes, outward acts matter too in the eyes of the law. But to Jesus, the intent within is equally serious. That's how much he values every woman. And as soon as we start seeing things his way, scary as it is, we'll start getting free. And the whole world will start getting better.

I've written to you about your glory and her glory. And, I'm thinking, enough is enough for this letter. So I'll finish by asking you to accept this key insight: *Every relationship is either Christlike or predatory.* There is no neutrality. But you *can* become Christlike, in heart and behavior, toward every woman on the face of the earth.

That's where we're going next. But let me warn you. As you grow in experiencing your royalty—and hers—the difference might feel shocking. One of my heroes, the Anglican bishop Festo Kivengere of Uganda, preaching in England years ago, told this true story about a man renewed by the risen Christ:

I could tell you a case of a man . . . back home, forty-five years old—a pagan, illiterate, who knew nothing about Christ. Then he was brought by grace, through the preaching of the Christians, into the presence of Jesus and Him crucified; and that man was so changed that within a month, when impure thoughts came into his heart, he literally went outside from a meeting and vomited. . . . What sensitivity! A man steeped in paganism, with no Bible training, no background. And now in the light of Calvary, . . . this man is taken, re-created, renewed, his conscience is so clean that when impure thoughts came, he even went and physically vomited. A sensitivity had been created. The Holy Spirit had renewed the personality. Is this your case?[8]

Your vomit doesn't wash away your sins. Only the blood of Jesus can do that. But it won't do you any harm at all to get sickened over your sins. Jesus said, "Blessed are those who mourn, for they shall be comforted" (Matt. 5:4).

It's sure better than shutting down our sensitivity, don't you think?

Because she matters,
Ray

---

8 Festo Kivengere, "Christ the Renewer," in *The Keswick Week 1972*, ed. H. F. Stevenson (London: Marshall, Morgan & Scott, 1972), 75.

3

He Is Royalty

Jesus matters too. Not the Jesus you might have pictured in your mind. But the industrial-strength Jesus who is actually there. He cares about the real you—and about her.

While we're at it, where *did* you get your idea of Jesus? Did it just rub off on you along the way? Or did you learn it from the Bible? There are many false Jesuses out there to defraud you, right where you need help the most.

For example, the "Feel-Good Jesus" is popular. He always smiles, always approves, never disagrees. He's just grateful when you show up in church now and then. And during your week, no matter what you do, you can always count on this Jesus to tell you it's going to be okay and everyone goes to heaven, because everyone is basically good at heart.

One tip-off that this false Jesus is sneaking into your thoughts is when you honestly wonder: *So what's all* that *bad with a little porn now and then, especially when life gets stressful? It's harmless, isn't it? And I'm no worse than the average guy. Maybe better than most. So Jesus is cool with me, right?*

But this bobblehead Jesus, small enough to fit anywhere, is no King. And in your saner moments, you know he can't be trusted. Conscience whispers to you that your problems are more serious than this Jesus Jr. seems to realize. Which is why the opposite Jesus—another false Jesus—can seem like a legit alternative: the "Feel-Bad Jesus."

At least, he's a serious voice. Let's give him that. But this tough hombre is always pointing out your shortcomings. Your best is never good enough. This harsh Jesus, so disappointed with you, rolls his eyes with a "Really? You did it *again*?" And what can you say?

But along with his faultfinding—his stick to beat you up—"Feel-Bad Jesus" also offers a carrot: if you'll just try harder, you might make the cut and stay out of hell. Put your mind to it, and you'll stand above other sinners—the unwashed godforsaken down in the gutters. He might even let you put on a robe and sing in his choir up in the clouds forever—the best version of heaven he has to offer.

Haven't you met people who believe in this false Jesus? I have. They seem miserable. But funny thing—they seem to *like* their miserable religion. Maybe it helps them feel superior? I don't know. But "Feel-Bad Jesus" is no King either. He's a smug phantom, dreamed up by our guilty fears. Good riddance!

Our self-invented Jesuses don't help us at all. If our next step is to open up to the real King who helps real sinners, the time has come to evict every mythical Jesus we've "accepted into our hearts."

Here's a surprising fact of history, Son. The real Jesus *attracted* failures, exiles, rejects, underachievers, weaklings, compromisers, and losers—the scum of the earth. Every kind of defeated, fed-up sinner found a welcome with him. It was the above-it-all religious elite who hated his guts. But the guilty, the unwashed? He didn't merely tolerate them; he *befriended* them. He wasn't exhausted by them; they *energized* him. He knew full well who they were, where they'd been, what they'd done and would do again—and what they would cost him. Yet he was *for* them, with all his heart.

———

And he is for *you*.

———

Right now, at this very moment, his heart moves not toward the strong but toward the broken. His tender heart for sinners was the very thing that stood out the most in the eyes of his critics. Here was a moral man, and immoral people felt *hopeful* around him. But to the uppity finger-pointers, being "a friend of sinners" was his crime. It was an accusation he gladly accepted.

Son, isn't that King *true* royalty?

What if I told you that every false Jesus we've ever believed in was whispered into our minds by Satan himself? Wouldn't that be just like Satan—keeping us far from the *real* Jesus, whose heart longs to give us everything a man desires in this world and beyond, who is eager to give us the rush of a fist-bumping *yes!* for every hard-won victory along the way?

Satan is happy for you to settle for the "Feel-Good Jesus"—one so weak in the knees and thin in the wallet that he doesn't even *know* how to help you get free of porn. Satan is equally happy for you to put up with the "Feel-Bad Jesus," who shames you and drives you back to porn for false comfort and real bondage.

What Satan *doesn't* want you to think about is who you really are, who she really is, and (most of all) who Jesus really is—your true King who wants you feeling like *a man*. A man with a clear conscience. A man who knows he's walking the right path. A man of integrity building a world of nobility. That man *refuses* to let his past rob him of his future. That man isn't getting pushed around anymore. He's pushing back and reaching for "newness of life" (Rom. 6:4).

It seems crazy, but it's true. *Every time you log on to a porn site, what you're really looking for is Jesus.*[1] There's a whole lot to him. Check this out:

1. Jesus Is a Conquering Lion

"Behold, the Lion of the tribe of Judah . . . has conquered" (Rev. 5:5). As our majestic and fearless King,[2] this Lion bounds into our world every day, rescuing more and more people from the demonic jackals and hyenas that prey upon the weak. His enemies might look strong. But before the Lion, they're helpless.

What's more, the Bible says the Lion "has conquered"—*already*. There's still a lot wrong with this world. We've never succeeded in eradicating evil. But Jesus has conquered forever.

Two thousand years ago—we're too late to undo his success—this world's top people crucified the most noble man who ever walked this earth. But on the third day, he exploded from that tomb, surging with life and power from above. Who's going to stop him now? So the future of this world is not up for grabs. Our King is the *only* one "on the right side of history."

It means a lot to me that Jesus owns this world. The wrongs done to us and the wrongs we ourselves do—what if they don't define us anymore? What if the Lion has conquered it all? What if he's bending our sufferings around so that they end up *enhancing* our royalty? Then there's no need for a cheap way to lick our wounds

---

1   With thanks to Bruce Marshall, *The World, the Flesh, and Father Smith* (Boston: Houghton Mifflin, 1945), 108.

2   The lion imagery comes from the messianic prophecy in Gen. 49:9–10. Bruce K. Waltke, *Genesis: A Commentary* (Grand Rapids, MI: Zondervan, 2001), 607: "This most powerful and daring beast of prey was a symbol of kingship in the ancient Near East."

or a quick fix to feel like a man again. Thanks to Jesus, all the evils tormenting us and our world are a spent force. Hidden behind the outward show is deep exhaustion. Injustice is bluffing. Every day the temptations of this world whisper to us, "Give up, and give in!" But our King made us a promise: "I will come again" (John 14:3). And on that final day, the Lion will devour every wrong and make everything right again—forever.

For us, that coming day will be like the moment in *The Lord of the Rings* when Sam wakes up, surprised to be alive and well in the land of Ithilien.

> Sam lay back, and stared with open mouth, and for a moment, between bewilderment and great joy, he could not answer. At last he gasped: "Gandalf! I thought you were dead! But then I thought I was dead myself. Is everything sad going to come untrue? What's happened to the world?"
>
> "A great shadow has departed," said Gandalf, and then he laughed, and the sound was like music, or like water in a parched land; and as he listened the thought came to Sam that he had not heard laughter, the pure sound of merriment, for days upon days without count. It fell upon his ears like the echo of all the joys he had ever known. But he himself burst into tears.[3]

Sometimes we wonder if our King's presence then will make up for our pain now. But C. S. Lewis wisely taught us, "Heaven, once attained, will work backwards and turn even that agony into a glory."[4] So we can relax. We can live with unmet needs. We can wait. He's worth the wait. The Lion guarantees the Golden Age foretold

---

3 J. R. R. Tolkien, *The Lord of the Rings: The Return of the King* (Boston: Houghton Mifflin, 1994), 930–31.

4 C. S. Lewis, *The Great Divorce* (New York: Simon and Schuster, 1996), 67.

by the prophets of old, and his new world will never end. In the meantime, he's got this. He's got us.

Jesus is our conquering Lion. But he is more. Surprisingly more.

2. Jesus Is a Slain Lamb

"I saw a Lamb standing, as though it had been slain" (Rev. 5:6). This striking vision, along with "Behold, the Lion of the tribe of Judah" (Rev. 5:5), shows us the grandeur of Jesus. He is not a simplistic, one-dimensional King. He is a conquering Lion and a slain Lamb. He isn't an either–or. And he isn't a compromise of two opposites mushed together. He is *both* a Lion *and* a Lamb—simultaneously, fully.[5]

As a slain Lamb, Jesus is the atoning sacrifice.[6] After all, *something* must be done to offset our sins. They don't just go *poof!*—by good luck or by good works. We're all trapped in consequences we didn't intend but we did create. And if *we* have to answer for what we've done, we have no future.

After years of denial, baseball legend Pete Rose finally admitted to betting on his games: "People have to understand I wish this would have never happened. But I can't change it, it's happened. And I'm just looking for a second chance." We get that, don't we? We look at episodes in our past and think: *If only I could relive those moments! If only I could trade in my record for a better one!*

This sadness we carry around is one reason we men sneak off into a Fantasyland of total "freedom." In that world, we can do whatever we want, with no consequences, nothing to answer

---

5 Jonathan Edwards, "The Excellency of Christ," in *The Works of Jonathan Edwards*, ed. Edward Hickman, 2 vols. (London, 1834; repr., Edinburgh: Banner of Truth, 1979), 1:680: "There is an admirable conjunction of diverse excellencies in Jesus Christ."

6 The lamb imagery comes from many Old Testament passages—the Passover lamb in Ex. 12:1–13, for example.

for. But Monday morning always rolls around. We have to get up, take out the trash, hustle to work, pay the bills, and so on. And this deeper question never goes away: *What is there in all this world that can make my sins go away—far enough away to leave me in peace?*

Jesus says to us, "I am the Lamb slain to answer for whatever you've done. Come to me, all who labor and are heavy laden, and I will give you rest."[7]

Corrie ten Boom, the Dutch survivor of a Nazi prison, understood our need. She said that when God casts our sins into the depths of the sea, he also puts up a sign: "No fishing allowed!"[8] How can our own shallow remedies compete with that?

It helps us that the roaring Lion and the sacrificial Lamb are one and the same person. He respects us enough to confront our sins. But he also values us enough to pay for our sins—at cost to himself alone. Jesus is building his new kingdom in a surprising way. He gives porn stars their dignity back, and he gives porn consumers their honor back. He *loves* doing this.

The Lion and the Lamb. For you. For me.

You and I have so much in common. The only big difference between us is that I've sinned a lot more than you have. I've been sinning for over seventy years! What do I do with that now? The same as you. All Jesus asks me to do, all I *can* do, is lay it down at

7 This illustration comes from Raymond C. Ortlund Jr., *Isaiah: God Saves Sinners* (Wheaton, IL: Crossway, 2005), 352–53.
8 Corrie ten Boom, *Tramp for the Lord* (Fort Washington, PA: Christian Literature Crusade, 1974), 55.

the foot of his cross. Then it isn't mine anymore. It's his forever. And I'm finally free to start growing into a man of integrity building a world of nobility. In Christ's presence, both you and I are finally free to grow. More about that in another letter.

For now, what I'm saying is this. The Lion who is also the Lamb is big enough for you and me and all this world. If he "needs" anything from us at all, it's only our exhaustion and failure and sorrow. What other options do we have?

I love The Chronicles of Narnia by C. S. Lewis. In one part, a girl named Jill bursts into an opening in a forest. She's thirsty. She spies a stream not far away. But she doesn't rush forward to throw her face into its refreshing current. She freezes in fear. A huge, golden lion is resting there in the sun right beside the stream.

"Are you not thirsty?" said the Lion.

"I'm *dying* of thirst," said Jill.

"Then drink," said the Lion.

"May I—could I—would you mind going away while I do?" said Jill.

The Lion answered this only by a look and a very low growl. And as Jill gazed at its motionless bulk, she realized that she might as well have asked the whole mountain to move aside for her convenience.

The delicious rippling noise of the stream was driving her nearly frantic. "Will you promise not to—do anything to me, if I do come?" said Jill.

"I make no promise," said the Lion.

Jill was so thirsty now that, without realizing it, she had come a step nearer. "*Do* you eat girls?" she said.

"I have swallowed up girls and boys, women and men, kings and emperors, cities and realms," said the Lion. It didn't say this as if it were boasting, nor as if it were sorry, nor as if it were angry. It just said it.

"I daren't come and drink," said Jill.

"Then you will die of thirst," said the Lion.

"Oh dear!" said Jill, coming another step nearer. "I suppose I must go and look for another stream then."

"There is no other stream," said the Lion.[9]

Son, porn is not the stream to satisfy your thirst. It does offer endless hyperarousals, each new one only a click away. But what porn always delivers, after the momentary rush, is the steep letdown of emptiness and self-hatred—with less and less real sex too.[10]

But this letter is about our true King. And I'm asking you to hand yourself over to him. Then he'll plunge your past under his own blood. And he will provide everything you're going to need—moment by moment—as he leads you into your future.

I'm not talking about you changing from your normal life to your normal life-with-church-on-Sundays. I'm talking about you choosing between *two different worlds*, each one competing with the other, each one inviting you in—and further in.

Let's take a closer look, as I wrap this up.

One world is dominated by Satan. He is Christ's rival, but not his equal. Satan is the ultimate wannabe. And you've got to hand it to him. The world he's building is an exciting place. Energy and passion galore. All the cool kids hang out here.

The Bible says, "The whole world lies in the power of the evil one" (1 John 5:19). *That* is why porn feels inevitable, why integrity

---

9 C. S. Lewis, *The Silver Chair* (New York: Collier, 1972), 16–17. Italics original.

10 Belinda Luscombe, "Porn and the Threat to Virility," *Time*, April 11, 2016. In C. S. Lewis, *The Screwtape Letters* (New York: HarperOne, 1996), 44, the senior devil explains to the apprentice devil, "An ever increasing craving for an ever diminishing pleasure is the formula."

feels impossible. But Satan doesn't really even care about sex. What he's grabbing for is *everything*—the total denial of Jesus, the total denial of the Bible, the total denial of everyone's dignity, so that the whole world sinks into compliant helplessness. That's what porn is really about. It is *total war* against Jesus, *total war* against every hope in your heart. Porn offers to turbocharge your sexuality. But it neutralizes your authority and freedom as a serious man. And not even because *you* matter. Satan wants you only as a pawn for making *Jesus* look like a failure. Don't you see what's happening? Satan is using porn, and a lot more, for spreading a world-encompassing atmosphere of intimidation. He even makes it attractive. But it's all lies. "To do its worst, evil needs to look its best. Evil has to spend a lot on makeup."[11] The devil sure doesn't want anyone noticing something else—the risen Jesus growing his rebel movement right here.

This other, new world is being created by the risen King. Jesus is no less than a second Adam, launching nothing less than a new human race, building nothing less than an eternal garden of Eden.[12] At this very moment, Jesus is sprinting through our exhausted world, gathering up despairing sinners left and right, breathing new life into them, and having a blast doing so. He *prefers* the most hopeless cases. Lucky for us, right?

So who can defeat him? He's better at saving than we are at sinning: "He has delivered us from the domain of darkness and transferred us to the kingdom of his beloved Son, in whom we have redemption, *the forgiveness of sins*" (Col. 1:13–14). The more we've sinned, the more we qualify!

---

11 Cornelius Plantinga Jr., *Not the Way It's Supposed to Be: A Breviary of Sin* (Grand Rapids, MI: Eerdmans, 1995), 98.

12 Alec Motyer, *Look to the Rock* (Leicester: Inter-Varsity Press, 1996), 125: "When the rightful King returns to Eden, all the energies, pent up while sin abounded and death reigned, will explode in an endless burgeoning as creation itself hastens to lay its tribute at the feet of Him whose right it is to reign."

His new kingdom of life is springing up everywhere—"a great multitude that no one could number, from every nation, from all tribes and peoples and languages" (Rev. 7:9). There's room in there for *any* man! Why not you?

Here's what you stand to gain. When the King returns, he's going to re-create our suffering world as a new earth where there's no pain, no boredom, no depression. Every color will be brighter, every aroma richer, every taste more mouth-watering, every sunset more dramatic. In his nuclear-powered presence, we will finally feel fully alive.[13]

It gets better. The culture creating that we human beings have been busy with throughout history—our King will restore and preserve and perfect the best of our world for us to enjoy together forever. "The glory and honor of the nations" will be brought into the holy city (Rev. 21:26). The music, the art, the dress, the humor, the dance, the rhythms, the accents, the stories of all our cultures—our King *values* all the glory and honor we've made. When he returns, he won't delete it. He'll redeem it. *Heaven will be human and "down to earth"*—more than Satan's world.

For example, we'll be able to listen to a joke without having to brace ourselves against a distasteful punch line. Every new joke will be funnier than anything we ever heard here. We will laugh our fool heads off, and Jesus himself will be loving every minute of it.

The moment you step into his eternal world, here's how it might go for you. Remember that our Lord did not say, "I go to prepare a place." What he said was "I go to prepare a place *for you*" (John 14:2). So when *you* show up, you won't look around and say: "Well, okay. I can get used to this. Whatever." You'll look around and say:

13 Edwards, "Heaven," in *Works*, 2:628, describing the five senses of our resurrected bodies, writes that "every perceptive faculty shall be an inlet of delight." I thank my son Dr. Eric Ortlund for drawing my attention to this portion of Edwards.

"No way! He thought of *me*. He understood *my* crazy heart." And you'll take off running—first of all, toward *him*. You'll hurl yourself into his arms with such abandon you might knock him over. He won't mind. You'll both get up, laughing. And you'll look into his eyes, and he'll look into your eyes, and he'll ask, "Would you like a hug?" And you'll say, "I sure would." And he'll wrap you up in the biggest bear hug you've ever felt. He'll say quietly: "Take as long as you want. I've got time." And you'll feel the healing start to flow down into your deepest pain. You'll start discovering what it really feels like to be human. So there you'll be, in his ginormous bear hug, for maybe a year. And when you feel ready, you'll stand up and say: "Thanks, Lord. That felt good." And he will smile, and you will smile—two royal figures, and dear friends forever.

The great thing right now about your future is this. Any time at all, by faith, you can go there in your mind. Paint the picture for the eyes of your heart. You'll get fresh energy for living nobly amid the ruins of this tragic world. You'll need it. But you'll *have* it—always. Satan's world is a lie. It's collapsing. The King's new world is real. It's rising. Savor that thought.

I love the scene in *The Shawshank Redemption* when Andy locks himself into that office and plays Mozart over the PA system. The convicts are held spellbound by that beauty coming from far beyond those prison walls.

Then Red's voice-over reminds us what a power hope can be, whatever we're locked into right now:

I have no idea to this day what them two Italian ladies were singin' about. . . . I like to think they were singin' about something so beautiful it *can't* be expressed in words, and makes your heart ache because of it. I tell you, those voices *soared*. Higher and farther than anybody in a gray place dares to dream. It was like some beautiful bird flapped into our drab little cage and made these walls dissolve away . . . and for the briefest of moments— every last man at Shawshank felt free.[14]

That freedom of heart is what your royalty feels like right here, right now, in this broken world. It's a sacred gift from your King. Never let it go!

Because he matters,
Ray

---

14 Frank Darabont, *The Shawshank Redemption: The Shooting Script* (New York: Newmarket, 2013), 63–64. Italics original.

PART 2

REIMAGINING
THE FUTURE

4

We Can Do This

Now let's get practical. What are you going to *do* with your royalty?

Yes, you're amazing. But I hope you're seeing that your royalty is not for yourself only. One way you're amazing is this: for liberating other men in your generation. You're a freed man, to free others. That's the gift Jesus has given you. And I'm asking, what are you going to do about it?

Let me start here: *You're more ready than you feel.* Before you were born, God began shaping you for your mission. He has been preparing you all your life to stand as a prophetic presence in our world of lies. He is even now nudging you toward the bold decisions you're going to make by the time you finish this book. He is committed to helping you get started, and he's committed to sustaining you for historic impact. Look what he said to another young man just like you facing tough odds:

> Before I formed you in the womb I knew you,
> and before you were born I consecrated you;
> I appointed you a prophet to the nations. (Jer. 1:5)

Dude, I almost feel sorry for the devil, with you here messing with his crumbling kingdom! It's not just that *history* will change because of you; *eternity* will be richer because you're here taking your stand. You don't need to wait for a better day. You can start now.

Here's the great thing about right now. Yes, the porn industry is enslaving women and men by the millions all over the world today. But the great thing is this. *It's Game Day!* The divine Coach has his team on the field. He's calling the big play. And he has put *you* into the game. You're not sitting it out, on the bench, wondering if he'll ever call your name. You're on the field, and his team is playing offense. That's all that matters. You don't care which play the Coach calls. All you care about is running his play the best you can. And when you're tired and battered and bruised, you don't mind. Good football players play hurt. They even *like* it that way. When a guy on the team is all dirty and sweaty and bleeding and sore, and he breaks from the huddle and trots up to the line to run yet another play, even his pain feels good. It's how he *knows* he's a real football player. And that's you—right now.

So with the team already on the field, moving the ball toward the goal line, your part is basically simple. Not easy, but simple. *Just get going.* Stop doing nothing, and start doing something. And your something is *whatever* you can do.

In letter 6, I'll offer a menu of options for "next steps." But for now, just settle into this confidence. As you step out and get involved, all along the way the risen Jesus will keep giving you everything you need for building his new world. Yes, you'll pay a price. Yes, you'll sometimes fail—or you'll feel like you're failing. But with his smile upon you, you'll be able to keep going, and keep going, and keep going, and never quit.

You're on the right side of history, Son, not because of your resolve but because of his resurrection. Your time is now, not ten years from now. Your task is before you, not on some distant horizon. I am confident about your future because of his future. He is why you are successful *before you even move a muscle.* So go ahead and accept his call to action, whatever he asks you to do.

Your fight is like the final months of World War II. On June 6, 1944, D-Day, Allied troops stormed the northern coast of France to liberate Europe from Nazi tyranny. Once those soldiers had heroically, ferociously established a beachhead, they started moving inland, gaining ground one blood-soaked mile after another. The fight dragged on until May 8, 1945, VE-Day—nearly a year later—when the German army finally surrendered. *But the war had been won eleven months before, when the Germans couldn't stop the Allied landings on D-Day.*[1]

To the guys who fought so hard from the beaches of France into the heart of Germany, no sacrifice along the way was a waste. They were fighting not just *for* victory but *in* victory.

In the same way, Jesus won the decisive battle for this whole world by his death and resurrection two thousand years ago. His death looked like defeat. But he came roaring back with new life forever. Who can stop him now? His final victory is inevitable— a whole new world of nobility. Yes, we're still in the fight. And it's hard. But you're on the winning side. No sacrifice is pointless. Every sacrifice contributes. You're serving his powerful cause, with his constant help. He will never leave you nor forsake you (Heb. 13:5).

The only question is this: In what practical ways will *you* keep the fight moving forward?

That's what this letter is about—you getting ready, in heart and mind, for *your* personal fight. Here are three steps that will help

---

1   Oscar Cullmann, *Christ and Time: The Primitive Christian Conception of Time and History* (London: SCM, 1952), 84–87.

you. They sure help me. One, what you're fighting for. Two, how you can fight well. Three, what winning will cost you.

1. What You're Fighting For

He who is noble plans noble things,
and on noble things he stands. (Isa. 32:8)

How's that for a forearm tattoo—one line on each arm?

Whatever Jesus tells you to do, it will never be shameful or sneaky. You will never have to bend the rules when you serve him. He is noble, he plans noble things, and he will call you to stand only for noble things—in fact, a whole new world of nobility.

I checked out that biblical word *noble* (used three times in one verse!). *Noble* here doesn't refer to an aristocratic upper class. It's about a heroic man's character, wherever he might be located socially. I love this biblical word—*noble*. Here's what the word actually means: a man's eagerness to do more than the bare minimum. This word describes a generous, wholehearted guy who gladly volunteers to do *all* that's best for others. He is the opposite of a foot-dragger or a penny-pincher. He's all-in. That's true nobility. And Son, that's *you*.

Another reason I love the word *noble* is how it offers wisdom. You will face two opposite temptations: cowardice and fanaticism. Cowardice makes a man want to keep his head down until the trouble blows over. Fanaticism, on the other hand, gets a guy trying to force change by any means necessary. Both cowardice and fanaticism are foolish. And the wise path of nobility isn't a compromise between the two. It's a third way entirely.

For example, cowards in the 1800s didn't have the stomach to confront American slavery. Fanatics got violent—like John Brown, who hoped to trigger a slave uprising by attacking Harpers Ferry. But the noble Abraham Lincoln shouldered the burdens of responsible leadership—and changed the course of history. See the difference? Rising to your nobility will position you for making a lasting impact that future generations can respect.

Remember, when you take up the fight against evil, you are *planning* a noble thing. You are *standing for* a noble thing. If you ever feel like a coward in the face of the battle, you can pivot immediately, turn from your fear back to Jesus, and brace yourself again for the fight. Or if you ever feel like a fanatic, you can do the same thing: pivot right then and there and turn away from your craziness, back to Jesus, and find a sensible path forward. Stay close to him, and you will be steadily unstoppable.

So your goal in life is neither to save your precious hide nor to assert your grandiosity. Your nobility means you're not holding back, because Jesus is not holding out. He'll keep giving you "grace upon grace" (John 1:16) as you keep turning to him with need upon need. His door is always open to you, because he too is noble.

Opposing porn will demand your best, but Jesus will keep giving you his best. You are not doomed to failure. He *will* bring down this wretched industry, and he *will* create a world of nobility—through *you*.

Always remember that. You'll *need* to remember it.

Defeating porn seems impossible, doesn't it? Its appeal is seductive, its reach widespread, its presence well-established. But here's the difference God makes. Underdog David went up against monster Goliath, and the story ended with a wildly lopsided win for David (1 Sam. 17). God *loves* to flip impossibilities into actualities to show us how real he is. He's not looking to "back a winner." His heart is drawn to lost causes, making sure they succeed in the end. For you and me, that's a game changer.

I can't explain how it works, *but even small faith makes big changes.* Jesus said, "For truly, I say to you, if you have faith like a grain of mustard seed, you will say to this mountain, 'Move from here to there,' and it will move" (Matt. 17:20). God isn't looking for super-heroes. He's looking for ordinary men who don't mind becoming living proof of *his* mountain-moving power (2 Cor. 12:9). And who wouldn't love to be part of that?

Yes, every day this crazy world will try like mad to make you feel small. But T. S. Eliot helps us see the truth: "In a world of fugitives, the person taking the opposite direction will appear to be running away."[2] And all the help you're going to need will keep coming down to you from the divine nobleman above *who is so proud of you!*

Many years ago, during the Vietnam War, an anti-war protester was trudging through the snow outside a corporation in Minnesota, holding up his sign and making his statement. Someone passing by mocked him: "Why are you out here? You'll never change them!" The young protester wisely replied: "I'm not out here to change them. I'm out here to keep them from changing me."

When you're fighting for a new world of nobility, just the fight itself *is* winning. You can do that. Let's do that together, every day for the rest of our lives—fighting for the nobility of our own souls, for starters.

2. How You Can Fight Well

> Guard[3] your heart with all vigilance,
>   for from it flow the springs of life. (Prov. 4:23)

Many people believe they'll flourish from the outside in, but we believe we flourish from the inside out. We believe the great things in life come not from our outward advantages but from our inward

---

2   T. S. Eliot, "The Family Reunion," in *The Complete Plays of T. S. Eliot* (New York: Houghton Mifflin Harcourt, 2014), 110.

3   My translation. The ESV reads, "*Keep* your heart . . . ," which is a correct translation. But "*Guard* your heart . . ." is also a valid rendering and conveys the force of the text more clearly. See NEB, NIV, REB, NLT.

resources. Which means that, however bad this world gets, with the risen Jesus living within you, you can always have something positive to offer everyone you meet.

His new world of nobility doesn't need you to look impressive. You *are* impressive. You just are. Don't worry about that. Concentrate instead on guarding your heart deep inside. Protect "with all vigilance" a clear conscience before the Lord. Remind yourself— even *announce* to yourself every day—that he rejoices over you. Whatever insanity is going on around you, his "springs of life" can flow within you and from you to refresh others.

A historian friend of mine—Dr. John Woodbridge—told me this true story about the great evangelist Billy Graham: In 1976 Jimmy Carter was running for the presidency. *Playboy* magazine interviewed him during the campaign. At one point in the interview, Carter admitted, "I've looked on a lot of women with lust. I've committed adultery in my heart many times."[4] That doesn't surprise us today, but it made national news then.

Not long after, Billy Graham was on the phone with my friend John. Among other things, they discussed the Carter interview. Billy explained how disappointed he was that a prominent Christian man would have to admit that. Billy wasn't naive, nor was he dumping on Carter. But he had set such a high standard for what he allowed into his own thought world that he was grieved for Carter. No wonder Billy Graham's ministry flowed with "the springs of life" for so many people![5]

Son, by God's grace, you can guard your heart with that same vigilance—in two ways.

---

4 Lee Dembart, "Carter's Comments on Sex Cause Concern," *New York Times*, September 23, 1976, https://www.nytimes.com/1976/09/23/archives/carters-comments-on-sex-cause -concern.html.

5 I thank Dr. Woodbridge for this account, given in a phone conversation, September 4, 2020.

One, you can guard your heart from lustful thoughts. Remember the high standard Jesus gave us? "Everyone who looks at a woman with lustful intent has already committed adultery with her in his heart" (Matt. 5:28). We have no right to say back to our King: "No. That's impossible. You're asking too much of me." His commands are not impossibilities—not with his help. Nor are his commands a menu of options we can choose from. His commands are his total integrity entering into us by his grace, making us whole.

Let's always say to him, "Lord, help me to obey you, right now, at a deeper level." And let's support one another as we fight for our integrity. But let's never make room for sin—even in our thoughts. The gospel calls us to live lives "fully pleasing to him" (Col. 1:10). That isn't sinless perfection. But it is total openness. It's what love for Jesus looks like. He loves us, and we love him back by giving him access to *all* that we are. And we *never* tell him to look away or back off or get out. We can face the worst within us, because he is our King of grace.

So the instant a lustful thought springs into our minds, let's *refuse* the temptation. And let's cry out to the Lord, "Help me!" He's always there. The Bible says of Job not that he was never tempted by evil but that he "turned away from evil" (Job 1:1, 8; 2:3). And the Bible calls that "integrity" (Job 2:9). It's like this. You can't stop birds from flying over your head, but you can stop them from making nests in your hair. That is what "guarding your heart" looks like. It's how "the springs of life" stay fresh and full within.

Two, you can guard your heart from despairing thoughts. Your worst temptation is not sexual but spiritual—giving up on God, because you think he's given up on you. Martin Luther understood.

My temptation is this—that I think I don't have a gracious God. This is [because I am still caught up in] the law. It is the greatest grief, and it produces death. God hates it, and he comforts us by saying, "I am your God." I know his promise. And yet, should some thought that isn't worth a fart nevertheless overwhelm me, I have the advantage (that our Lord God gives me) of taking hold of his Word once again. God be praised, I grasp the First Commandment which declares, "I am your God. I'm not going to devour you. I'm not going to poison you." . . . We ought to know that above all righteousness and above all sin stands the declaration, "I am the Lord your God."[6]

It is to us sinners that Jesus keeps offering himself: "Whoever believes in me"—not "whoever deserves me"—but "whoever *believes* in me, as the Scripture has said, 'Out of his heart will flow rivers of living water'" (John 7:38). So we're no longer limited to ourselves. We will never bring our need to Jesus and come away empty. I know this from experience, Son. You keep turning to him, and you'll know it from your own experience, more and more.

Here's how personal it gets. For too many years, I didn't understand why God created me sexual. This male sexual intensity I began to feel in my boyhood, which grew with my adult manhood and has been surging within me all these years—*why?* It can't be dirty. It can't be absurd. It was his idea. But what was his purpose?

At some point along the way it finally dawned on me: "Oh, my strong feelings aren't just for *me*. They're for *her*. My sexuality burns within me to drive me to my wife, to make *her* happy."

For me as a married man, guarding my heart means devoting my sexuality—*all* this energy—to my wife, and to her only. Then my drive is focused and intensified all the more. That way my

6 Martin Luther, *Tabletalk*, ed. and trans. Theodore G. Tappert, vol. 54 of *Luther's Works*, ed. Jaroslav Pelikan and Helmut T. Lehmann (Philadelphia: Fortress, 1967), 75.

wife is honored and loved, and I'm honored and loved, and we as a couple have that much more positive energy for serving others. For us, this is how the human sexual drama flows into the "rivers of living water" Jesus promised.

Guarding our hearts is how, by his grace, my wife and I have found our way into a deep romance, with four kids and fifteen grandchildren to show for it. Jesus is building something of his new world of nobility through our family. It began when he touched my body with the gift of sexuality. But it began *making sense* when I finally received it as a gift not just to me but for *her*. Sexuality and spirituality can converge with life-giving power. Who knew?

Son, during your single years, and during your married years when you're far from home, your sexuality can still be powerful for good. Inactive sexuality is not nonsexuality. It is purposeful sexuality. It is sexuality finding its ultimate purpose, dedicated to God—and blessed by God. How do we know? How do we know that inactive sexuality can be glorious sexuality? We know from Jesus. He was a man, he never had sex, and he was gloriously complete. What did he do with all his energies at all levels of his being? "He went about doing good" (Acts 10:38). So can you, by his grace, for his glory.

I'm not saying it's easy. It's hard. In fact, I know of only one thing harder than obeying the Lord, and that is *not* obeying the Lord. Caving to my impulses. Doing sexuality my own crazy way. And then feeling the bitter aftertaste of regret and shame. *That's* harder.

So why not receive your sexuality as a gift from him, and for him? Why not thank him for this amazing gift? Why not devote your sexuality to him every day? Guard your heart's understanding of his ennobling purpose for *all* that you are.

Your heart is your scariest danger but also your secret resource. The way to fight well over the long haul is by bringing your empty, broken heart to be filled and refilled, over and over again, by the Lord. You sure don't have to guard your heart from him! You can take your questions and sorrows and needs and confusion to him moment by moment. Open your Bible each morning, read a psalm, journal, and pray. Psalm 25, for example. It's real and raw. It's "living water" for exhausted men. Go there, take a deep dive one verse at a time, and Jesus will surprise you with how his heart can flow into your heart. He will *gladly* give you all you need for yourself and for others every day, until your dying day.

And when your time does come, you'll die happy. Your life will be an inspiring story of Jesus rescuing and refreshing others *through you*. At your funeral, people will weep. And the very memory of you will strengthen them for many more years, until *their* dying day.

3. What Winning Will Cost You

If by the Spirit you put to death the deeds of the body, you will live. (Rom. 8:13)

Like me, you've got some bad thoughts and feelings inside. They can't be managed or contained—or long concealed. Like me, you've tried your own halfway measures. And nothing has worked, right? Then you know what needs to happen.

Those parts of you that keep dragging you down must *die*—maybe a thousand times.

A big part of getting ready for your fight is turning the darkest places within you over to the Holy Spirit. He knows them all anyway. And he won't belittle you. The worst parts of you are, in fact, where he loves you the most. But the time has come for you to put to death, with his help, that one sin that keeps you from going all-in with Jesus. You're overdue for holding a very personal funeral. The Spirit will give you the courage and the wisdom to fight and fight and fight, until you win.

"Putting to death the deeds of the body," for me, starts with mental alertness every day. Sometimes it gets intense.

Several years ago I was writing a book on marriage and found myself in a constant struggle within. No one could have guessed. I didn't act out—thank the Lord. But the raging battle in my thoughts, the intrusive temptations in my mind—it was like hand-to-hand combat every day. As I was writing a book on *marriage*! When the book was finally completed, somehow the intensity just faded away. I guess I won.

All I could do was thank my mighty Ally, the Holy Spirit, for getting me through. But I didn't break out the champagne. I was just *relieved*. For me, "putting to death the deeds of the body" wasn't like a Super Bowl championship victory with a gala celebration afterward. It was more like the clouds parting, the sun breaking through, and calm descending, finally leaving me in peace. The temptations had kept on assaulting me, but I kept on crying out to the Lord. It wasn't a technique I mastered. It was just cold fear driving me to Christ time after time. And he held onto me. It felt like it would never end. But it did end. He made sure of that. So I laid my wreath of victory at his feet, for sure, because my part in it all was simple—just to keep turning to him, moment by moment.

You have your own stories to tell about how he has helped you too. And we'll be swapping our war stories like this at parties in heaven for a long, long time. And then we *will* break out the champagne! But for now, let's keep fighting as if our very lives depend on it, because they do. Let's cling stubbornly to Jesus as our only hope, because he is. And we have his Spirit to help us "put to death the deeds of the body." He's good at it.

C. S. Lewis, in his book *The Great Divorce*, paints the picture of our Lord's redemptive killing-power. The story he tells—and it's a great one!—goes like this: Some people from hell are allowed to take a bus trip up to the outskirts of heaven to see if they'd like to stay. They get off the bus and find themselves in a beautiful valley, with heaven just over the mountains to the east. The visitors from hell are surprised that, compared with how normal they looked back down below, now they seem faded, like ghosts. And the heavenly beings who come to talk with them are solid and big and radiant.

At one point in the story, a man from hell is walking around carrying one particular sin: lust. It's a little red lizard sitting on his shoulder, flicking its tail and whispering lies in his ear. You can tell the guy hates the embarrassment of it, hates its annoying chatter, but he won't let it go. It's a can't-live-*with*-him, can't-live-*without*-him kind of thing. So the man turns away from the mountains, keeping his distance from heaven.

A voice calls to him, "Off so soon?" It's an angel! The man admits that, yes, his pet ("this little chap," he calls him) doesn't really belong up here. The lizard had promised to keep quiet on the trip, he says, but the thing just won't shut up. So they're heading back down to hell, where they belong.

"Would you like me to make him quiet?" the angel asks.

"Of course, I would," the ghost answers, honestly.

"Then I will kill him," says the angel, stepping forward, ready to act immediately. The ghost freaks out, falling back with a howl of fright. He isn't ready for anything as drastic as *killing* his little darling!

What plays out then, for quite a while, is the man bobbing and weaving with excuses and evasions, while the angel sincerely, repeatedly offers to kill the wretched lizard.

"Don't you *want* him dead?" the angel presses him. *Well, uh . . .*

"It's the only way," the angel explains. *Gee, really? I'm not so sure . . .*

"May I kill it?" the angel asks again and again. But the guy can't believe he needs such an extreme remedy. He wants his little pet quiet and tame—but not dead. Yet the angel keeps insisting there is no other way. So, "May I kill it?"

Finally, the man gets angry, defensive. His feelings are hurt. The angel is humiliating him, he says. Making fun of him, he says. Trying to pressure him, he says, into doing something against his will. *Not at all*, the angel says. "I cannot kill it against your will." But it can be over—with one bone-crushing decision.

Okay then! the man finally gives in and agrees—with a whimper. "Go on. Do what you like. Just get it over with," though he's terrified at being separated from his little pleasure.

With a sudden twist of his mighty hands, the angel squeezes the breath out of the filthy lizard, flinging its lifeless body to the ground. The man reels, screaming in agony, as if dying himself.

All becomes still. Is that the end of it? Both of them dead? No. Suddenly, that very man who'd been weak and whining stands boldly to his feet. A *new* man—noble, formidable, chiseled with strength, radiant with glory. And the lizard? Far from dying, it too rises into something new—a white stallion, rippling with flesh and muscle, shaking its golden mane, greeting the new man as his mighty servant.

More swiftly than the storyteller can explain, man and horse head off at a full gallop, not back toward hell but onward toward heaven, over the mountains, climbing impossible steeps, "quicker every moment, till near the dim brow of the landscape, so high that I must strain my neck to see them, they vanished, bright themselves, into the rose-brightness of that everlasting morning."[7]

Son, whatever the Spirit kills in you, he also raises to newness of life, better than before. He isn't asking you to lose your sexuality.

---

7   C. S. Lewis, *The Great Divorce* (New York: Simon and Schuster, 1996), 96–101. Italics original.

He's asking you to gain your true sexuality—your glorious, purposeful, life-giving, manly sexuality. The lust you hesitate to part with is a lizard-like, bizarre, wannabe sexuality, a little souvenir from Fantasyland that lies to you and keeps you locked in shame. But putting it to death by the Holy Spirit's life-giving power means the real thrill can be yours, Son—the uplifting thrill of re-centering your life around planning noble things, standing for noble things, starting with your sexuality. Jesus died and rose again to give you nothing less than a magnificent new you. But you can't drag your old fantasies into his newness. They've got to die. They deserve to die. And the time is now.

What do you have to lose? That lizardy sexuality pampering you, whispering its enticements—kill it, as often as you need to. Ask the Holy Spirit to help you. *He will.*

Then, however Jesus calls you to fight for his new world of nobility, you'll be free to answer the call—joyously, decisively, repeatedly.

Because you're ready,
Ray

5

We Can Work Together

DEAR SON,

You won't regain your integrity all by yourself alone. But you can flourish—any man can flourish—in strong brotherhood with other men. Your life will count big-time as you become part of a vast army.

You don't need to be superhuman. You can be the stumbler that you are, a stumbler like me. But the thing about us is that we stumble together toward Jesus. And he makes us mighty. That's how you, with your brothers, will create a new world of nobility. *Moving forward shoulder to shoulder, you can starve that predatory Beast—the porn industry.*

My dear dad understood: "To choose to be alone is to invite sure failure."[1] And here's *why* flying solo will inevitably crash. What we're up against is not just this problem over here and that issue over there. What's gone wrong is nothing less than a whole culture of abuse and rape. What we need now is nothing less than

---

1 Raymond C. Ortlund, *Lord, Make My Life a Miracle!* (Ventura, CA: Regal, 1974), 60.

a growing counterculture of integrity and nobility. That's how the impact of your life can reach historic magnitude. You *can* build that new world of nobility.

But not by your own swagger and pushiness. God will succeed by his weak and foolish strategy—the cross (1 Cor. 1:25). Your first step, then, is to let Jesus be the only hero in your story. Once that's settled, simply get going. Start small, and grow it from there. Start gathering with other men, and keep recruiting new guys, and slowly enlarge the circle of brotherhood. Many men are longing to live for something inspiring. Offer it to them.

In this letter, I want to paint the picture of that new brotherhood. I'm not talking about "accountability," as some men practice it. Accountability can be coercive, bossy, impatient, shaming, and clumsy. I hate that. Neither am I talking about any formulaic method for improving ourselves and saving the world. Real progress is not simple or automatic. What helps one guy might not help another guy. But Jesus offers wisdom from God to empower all men, whoever they are. In other words, "Help and change follow a path, not a script."[2]

So let me describe the path that can help you and every man you know—real brotherhood breathing oxygen into exhausted guys, inspiring hope in defeated guys, putting confidence into skeptical guys. And the sky's the limit to what they can accomplish.

Together, "striving side by side" (Phil. 1:27), you can start experiencing not just community but a new *kind* of community—deep belonging and gentle safety in a world of posing and hiding. But men who dare to open up and become honest with one another— if you jump into this, Son, it might be your most life-giving experience yet. *Jesus himself will be there among you.* He doesn't hang out

---

2 "Who Is CCEF?" (brochure, 2020), point 5. The Christian Counseling and Educational Foundation in Philadelphia is a rich resource for understanding how life actually works. See https://www.ccef.org.

with the big shots and heavy hitters. But he *loves* to draw near to the men who've hit rock bottom,

> to revive the spirit of the lowly,
>   and to revive the heart of the contrite. (Isa. 57:15)

Go down low. He's waiting for you there. Bring other guys with you. Jesus will refresh you all. And he will send you and your brothers out on his mission to "let the broken victims go free" (Luke 4:18 REB).

Here's why *you cannot possibly fail.* Jesus builds his new world of nobility not by men parading their virtues but by men admitting their failings. All we need, in order to qualify with him, is to be done with pretending. I'm so done with it. I think you are too.

Here's the key Scripture to guide us into his new brotherhood: "Therefore, confess your sins to one another, and pray for one another, that you may be healed" (James 5:16).

Three things stand out here: confession, prayer, healing. When we sinful men come out of hiding, God's power comes down, and healing starts spreading out from there.

1. Confession

We don't overcome our sins by heroic willpower. We *confess* them to death. "Therefore, confess your sins to one another"—it's our fast track to healing. So let's swallow our pride. Let's start confessing and keep on confessing[3] to a brother, who starts praying and keeps on praying, until God's healing power comes down to us, and to others around us, to the ends of the earth.

---

3   E. H. Plumptre, *The General Epistle of St. James* (Cambridge: Cambridge University Press, 1901), 105: "The tense of the imperatives implies continuous action."

Taking the plunge can be hard. Really hard. My son Gavin, after reading *The Four Loves* by C. S. Lewis, said it well: "Sexual love requires you to take your clothes off. Friendship love requires you to do something harder—take your mask off." It's humiliating to admit how we're *really* doing, isn't it? But if you're going to change, if the world is going to change, it starts right here with us, confessing our sins. One other man, at least, *must* know what isn't working in your life and what you're really facing deep inside. Who is that guy you can trust at a deep level? Who is that solid brother in your city or town you can safely talk to about how you're failing most painfully?

That's how we defy our shame. *That's* how freedom moves in and starts taking over. By confessing our real sins to our real brothers, we discover how *gentle* Jesus is with broken men who are finally ready for healing. His reassuring kindness, made visible to you in your brothers, is why you really can come out of hiding and never go back there again.

Confessing your sins to Jesus alone isn't that hard, is it? It's a good thing to do, don't get me wrong. But does private confession to him alone free you all that much? Confessing your sins openly to brothers you respect—that's different. It's like *dying*. It destroys the false self you've been projecting. But when you start revealing the sin-sick man you really are, Jesus himself becomes more real. And you become more real. And brotherhood becomes more real. You exhale and relax, because you finally *belong*. And porn starts losing its grip.

"Confess your sins to one another" raises one obvious question: *To whom do you confess your sins?* Maybe you don't believe in Confession the way the Roman Catholic Church practices it. Okay. But how *will* you confess your sins? You're either confessing them or suppressing them. Which of those two strategies will actually *help* you? Which of those two will help *the world?*

The very fact that we hold back from honesty with one another—that itself is worth noticing. Shame has binding power. Sin offers the bait, but it hides the hook. The pleasure lasts briefly, but the regret lingers long. We know enough Christianity to feel bad about our sins, but we haven't gone far enough with Jesus to feel forgiven. What finally sets us free is no mystery. It's right here in plain language: "Confess your sins to one another."

Here's why you can take the dare. That one sin that has sunk its claws into you and won't let you go—*that* sin, your *worst* sin, Jesus bled to wash it away. That episode of failure, that moment of betrayal—that's where he loves you not the least but the most. Jesus is not a life coach for winners who want to improve their game; he is the rescuer of losers who are squandering their chance at life. He turns selfish predators into noble rescuers. Only he can do this. And he *loves* doing it. He longs to do it for you—and for every man you know.

When we sinful men come together in Christ's presence for confession, he unites us as the brotherhood of his cross. Our most inexcusable sin, once nailed to his blood-soaked cross, loses its damning power forever. Are you a sinner but trusting in Jesus? Then you're not going to hell anymore! You face no condemnation (Rom. 8:1). So you can face anything now. We can face it together as brothers, hiding nothing from him or from one another. Isn't this the breathing space you long for?

Son, you can be impressive, or you can be known, but you can't be both. And if you choose to remain impressive while you're shoving your real sins down out of sight, not only do you remain unknown to other men who could help you, but also you start morphing into a different man yourself. As the years go by, any man who leaves room in his soul for porn starts becoming an *enemy* of integrity. He hardens into an *ally* of the porn industry, even while he thinks of himself as a decent guy. But his every click suppresses the cries of pain rising from the human suffering there. He doesn't realize he's telling those sufferers to shut up, he's telling his brothers to back off, and he's telling Jesus himself to look the other way—until he's gone so far he *can't* stop.

Son, you don't want to become that man. The time to get free is *now*!

Who then is that Christian brother you know, a man who isn't out for himself, to whom you can and must confess your sins? And I don't mean occasionally, when things get bad enough, but regularly, weekly. Decide now to make honest confession your "new normal." You will hear the voice of Jesus, through your brother, saying to you afresh: "Neither do I condemn you. Go now and leave your life of sin" (John 8:11 NIV). You'll feel like a new man. Ultimately, little by little, the whole world will start feeling new again. The weakness of honesty is your superpower that the lies of porn cannot defeat.

In his classic book *Life Together*, Dietrich Bonhoeffer guides us into this life-giving brotherhood. Here are some game-film highlights of the key section:

- Confession is our breakthrough to experiencing real brotherhood.
- But sin wants to keep a man by himself, withdrawn and alone.
- The more isolated a man is, the more destructive his sin becomes.
- By confession, the light of the gospel can shine into his dark places.
- When a man finally surrenders and opens up, his sin starts weakening.
- The man receiving a brother's confession starts bearing his sin with him.
- Now both men are honest sinners, in deep brotherhood.
- A man living in ongoing confession will never be alone again.[4]

---

4 Dietrich Bonhoeffer, *Life Together* (New York: Harper, 1954), 112–13.

Why not spend the rest of your life building this liberating brotherhood with other guys *everywhere you go*?

Start today. Go ahead and call that brother you trust. Tell him what you're longing for. Tell him about James 5:16. Ask him if he'll let you confess your sins to him. Yes, be that blunt. And invite him to confess his sins to you. Assure him that everything you talk about will stay locked in the vault of your friendship, as a matter of sacred trust.[5] He will gladly agree, because he will feel trusted and honored. Then the two of you get together as soon as possible.

When you meet, don't waste time. Get right to the point. Read James 5:16 out loud. Then say to your brother, "Here are my worst sins this week." And put it out there, the embarrassing whole of it, until you have nothing left to hide. Then say to him, "So please pray for me." He will.

Then turn it around. He says to you, "And here's my mess." He lays it all out there. And then, "Please pray for me." You will.

Then maybe read together a passage like Psalm 32 or Isaiah 55:6–7 or John 8:2–11. And exhale. And rest. And give thanks. You're both in the Lord's kind hands now.

How can that not go well?

Finally, commit to a time the next week when you'll meet again. As you part company, you'll both be walking a new path, filled with new integrity and growing nobility.

It isn't rocket science. It's simple. It's got to be simple if it's going to work for us. The hardest part is swallowing our pride, right? But the awakening we long to see in our generation won't start with the porn stars owning up to the bad things they're

---

5   It might be legally necessary to inform the police of what a man confesses. Or it might be biblically necessary to inform church leaders of what a man confesses. Such a disclosure rarely becomes necessary. But this complete openness is part of men of integrity building a world of nobility.

displaying. It will start with us Christian guys owning up to the bad things we're concealing. *We are the holdouts. But we can also be the breakouts.*

2. Prayer

Here's the next step. Again, James 5:16 says, "Therefore, confess your sins to one another, *and pray for one another*, that you may be healed." We pray, because integrity is a miracle. So what does that kind of praying look like?

The verse doesn't say "fix one another" or even "advise one another," though good advice can help. But God wants us to *pray*. The verse goes on to say, "The *prayer* of a righteous person has great power as it is working." We don't have that power. God does. And he gives it to weak men who pray.

Prayer doesn't strike us as powerful. But it's how we experience what only God can do. A brother's prayer has great power as it is *working*, the Bible says here. The next verse puts before us Exhibit A—a weak man like us who got down to business with God: "Elijah was a man with a nature like ours, and he prayed *fervently*" (James 5:17). And it worked!

This kind of praying is preapproved. God likes it. He's not hoping your prayers might be eloquent. With God, all you have to be is desperate. Your prayers for one another as brothers can be as simple as this:

Lord, I'm here with my brother. He's a mess, and so am I. But you love us. So we're turning to you.

My brother has just confessed a serious sin. He's scared. So am I. But you sent Jesus to die a serious death for us. And what we want is not just to be forgiven. We want to become men of integrity building a world of nobility.

We want to weaken the serious evil preying upon us and our world—the porn industry. But how can we free others if we're still enslaved ourselves? Lord, free my brother! Empower him with more grace than he's ever known before! Make him a mighty force to bring down strongholds of oppression! Turn him around! Then he can lead *many* wounded people into green pastures and beside still waters!

And Lord, by asking you for this, I'm telling you it's what I want too. I'm all-in with my brother. You will never leave him nor forsake him, and neither will I. So you haven't heard the last from me about this. I will *never* quit on my brother.

So, there it is, Lord. That's my prayer. Thank you. In the holy name of Christ. Amen.

You don't have to use these words, obviously. What counts is your sincerity. But any guy can pray fervently—if he believes in God, and loves his brother, and wants to make the world a better place. God has *promised* his healing power in answer to our prayers.

Which leads us to the third takeaway here.

3. Healing

"Therefore, confess your sins to one another, and pray for one another, *that you may be healed.*" We don't need scolding, but we sure need healing—miraculous healing from above. It's what God *loves* to give to men who are fed up with their pampered selfishness.

Yes, James 5:16 is about the healing of our literal, physical diseases. We know that from verses 14–15. But verses 17–18 broaden the healing power of prayer to our sicknesses of soul, all our wounds and traumas, our deepest anguish and regrets—

everything that holds us back.[6] And there is no end to the healings God can give.

For example—what if, in answer to prayer, you start feeling forgiven by God? How healing! What if, in answer to prayer, you start feeling clean inside, like a kid again? More healing! What if, in answer to prayer, you get excited about your future again? Still more healing! What if, in answer to prayer, the shaming voice within, telling you you're worthless, shuts its lying mouth because the Holy Spirit is telling you you're significant? Mega-healing!

An honest man in a praying brotherhood is located right where God has promised his gentle healing will flow. And that man and his brothers together become a healing movement in our suffering world. Now that's a cause we can get behind, can't we?

What if, over the next ten years, our risen King gathers men all over the world into small groups for a new lifestyle of honest confession and healing prayer? What if his life-giving power starts flowing out through those men to heal many others? What if a mighty wave of healing from above washes over *all* of us? What if a new world of nobility starts at the low end and moves up? What if, down where everyone least expects it, our King shows up with grace and mercy for the very ones who see themselves as dirty and damned? What if, ten years from now, we're all looking around and saying, "Man, I didn't see *that* coming!" *What if Jesus visits us with a cleansing, a refreshing, a joy that right now we don't even believe is real?*

Son, you can be part of that miracle. Don't think for a moment God can't heal you. Try him out. Put James 5:16 to the test. You will be surprised at what starts stirring in you as you pour out your mess in confession and you hear a brother praying and praying and

---

6 Thomas Manton, *A Commentary on James* (Edinburgh: Banner of Truth, 1988), 462: "*That you may be healed*: The word *healed* is widely used and implies freedom from the diseases of either soul or body, and the context allows for both." Style updated.

praying for you. God's new world of nobility will start becoming real—right where you are.

But it begins humbly, even embarrassingly. You come clean with your brother, confessing your sins, with plain language, withholding nothing. Your brother listens. He doesn't interrupt. He might weep. But he listens quietly until you're finished. Then he gently asks, "Is there anything else?" If there's more, you keep going, until you have nothing left to hide. It isn't easy, especially if you've never allowed anyone into your heart like that. But you won't die. You'll feel relieved, even hopeful. And then your brother might get down on his knees, and he'll pray. He'll pray fervently for you not just to be better behaved but to be healed, freed, alive again by the power of Jesus.

And history will start to change. Why? Because when we get real with the Lord, he gets real with us. His mighty heart is moved by our broken hearts and our simple prayers. And he will move toward you and start touching your places of deepest pain, the way Jesus touched that man with leprosy so long ago (Mark 1:41). The man's disease had left him disfigured, but Jesus wasn't disgusted. The disease made the man repulsive, but Jesus wasn't repelled. The power of the man's sickness could've easily spread to others, but the power of Jesus's healing easily spread to that man. What made the difference? Jesus, the Bible says, was "moved with pity."

His heart hasn't changed. Your need hasn't changed. And by yourself, you will never change. But your brother's prayer brings the Healer near, right where you need him the most. So—try him out?

Satan gloats when your conscience punishes you mercilessly. The more shame you feel, the more you're immobilized, and then you'll never have the courage to fight. But God wants your conscience clear and defiant. So here's some wisdom from Martin Luther, who knew how to fight shame. When the old accusing thoughts come back and want to rob you of your confidence, Luther explains how to shove the devil's accusations right back down his rotten throat:

> When the devil tells us we are sinners and therefore damned, we may answer, "Because you say I am a sinner, I will be righteous and saved." Then the devil will say, "No, you will be damned." And I will reply, "No, for I fly to Christ, who has given himself for my sins. Therefore, Satan, you will not prevail against me when you try to terrify me by telling me how great my sins are and try to reduce me to heaviness, distrust, despair, hatred, contempt and blasphemy. On the contrary, when you say I am a sinner, you give me armor and weapons against yourself, so that I can cut your throat with your own sword and tread you under my feet, for Christ died for sinners. My sin is on his shoulders, not mine. So when you say I am a sinner, you do not terrify me but you comfort me immeasurably."[7]

Son, never grovel before that sorry loser, that lying wretch, your enemy the devil! By your stubborn faith in Christ, stand up for your hard-won freedom. Again, Martin Luther teaches us what to do:

> When the devil throws our sins up to us and declares that we deserve death and hell, we ought to speak thus: "I admit that I deserve death and hell. What of it? Does this mean that I shall be sentenced to eternal damnation? By no means. For I know One who suffered and made satisfaction in my behalf. His name is Jesus Christ, the Son of God. Where he is, there I shall be also."[8]

---

7   Martin Luther, *Galatians* (Wheaton, IL: Crossway, 1998), 40–41.
8   Theodore G. Tappert, ed., *Luther: Letters of Spiritual Counsel* (Philadelphia: Westminster, 1955), 86–87.

What can Satan say to that? And you keep moving forward with confession and prayer. Go for it, you gospel Jedi!

In this life, your healing won't be perfect. You'll have setbacks. But with Jesus, even your failures will end up making you more battle-hardened, more determined, more unstoppable. Walking in his ways, you and other men of integrity *will* build his world of nobility.

So you have Jesus. You have your brother. You have prayer. Now start experiencing God's healing power!

It gets even better—deeper and wider. Let me paint the picture.

As you experience real brotherhood with one other man, the two of you start dreaming about bringing in other guys. Tell them about what the two of you are experiencing. Tell the story of the courageous new steps you're taking. Most guys will be intrigued. All around you are men who are ready right now to band together and get real and make a difference. Find out who those guys are, and bring them in.

When your group starts meeting, sit in a circle together, not in rows like a classroom. It will help if you gently facilitate. You'll know when to speak and guide, and when to keep quiet and let it roll.

Your goal is that when the meeting is over, every man walks out with two fresh experiences: *one*, he has unburdened his heart and been prayed for; *two*, he has listened to the other guys unburdening their hearts and has prayed for them. Every man receives help, and every man gives help. No man hogs the time, and no man is left out.

As you begin your time together, welcome the guys and start out with an encouraging verse from the Bible. Not a Bible lecture. The fewer your words, the better. Just open up your Bible and read one super-encouraging promise there. Psalm 34:18, for example:

The LORD is near to the brokenhearted
and saves the crushed in spirit.

In one sentence, tell the guys what you love about that verse, how it helps you. Then invite them to add their thoughts. Then ask somebody to pray, inviting God's felt presence in among you. The last thing, to get going, is you reading James 5:16 as the only agenda for your meeting. Then you open it up with, "Okay, who's first?" And the brotherhood takes off!

Back when the First Great Awakening was sweeping over the world, the leaders gathered people together in small groups like the one I'm suggesting. They drew up some "ground rules" for how these small groups could help people really come alive. Here's one: "That every one, in order, speak as freely, plainly and concisely as he can the real State of his Heart, with his several Temptations and Deliverances, since the last time of meeting."[9]

What made the experience amazing was not the rules but the real state of their hearts. And they weren't spiraling down into whiney navel-gazing. Yes, they talked about their temptations. But they also talked about their deliverances—how the Lord was helping them. That's important. Real brotherhood is more than human empathy. It's divine miracle. No wonder it goes viral!

Your brotherhood can go viral. It can easily multiply, leaping over barriers, reaching men far away, men you might never even meet in this life. But in our sick world, healing is a powerful force. Your new freedom of heart can flow out, by the grace of God, reaching even the darkest places of porn. *God* can do that through you—the real you, with other real men.

---

9   John Simon, *John Wesley and the Religious Societies* (London: Epworth, 1921), 196–98, quoted in Raymond C. Ortlund, *Let the Church Be the Church* (Waco, TX: Word, 1983), 75.

Oh, one more quick thing. But it matters. Save some space toward the end of your gathering for "honor time." The Bible says, "Outdo one another in showing honor" (Rom. 12:10). It's competitive, but *everyone* wins. I'm not talking about flattery but real honoring of one another. So you say: "Okay, guys, before we go, one more thing. The Bible says, 'Outdo one another in showing honor.' Every guy here is an honorable man, and it's obvious. We see it all the time. So let's talk about it. Who's first?" And a guy might start out like this: "Jim, last Thursday night when I felt like looking at porn, and I texted you, you called me, and we talked until I was able to back away from the edge of that pit. Thank you, Jim. I honor you." And Jim might reply, "No, I honor *you*! You had the integrity to text me. Man, do you realize how much every man here respects that? Way to go!"

When guys are honest and prayed for and strengthened with mutual honor—you might find it hard to shut it down. It's so powerful!

Why not call a brother right now and get started?

Because you belong,
Ray

6

We Can Make a World of Difference

DEAR SON,

I'll start my final letter with a question for both of us: "In these days of exceptional evil, are you doing something exceptional? Or are you just content with doing some routine things?"[1] Let's do something exceptional—whatever the cost.

You and your brothers certainly have an exceptional task before you. Jesus is calling you to build *a new world of nobility*, to the furthest extent of your influence, for the rest of your life. And he's in the fight with you. He has no Plan B, in case you wreck Plan A. He doesn't need you to make him successful. He has set his own happiness on *your* success.

Not only that—this is amazing to me—but Jesus is already present in your future. You and I live inside these tiny increments of reality called "the present moment." But in his eternality, he is equally present to all points of time at once. So day by day he'll welcome your arrival, eager to help as you move forward for him.

---

1 Martyn Lloyd-Jones, *Revival* (Westchester, IL: Crossway, 1987), 169–70.

And since he's there in your future right now, ready for you, why hold back?

This letter describes some paths you can take for building his new world. It's a list of options and far from complete. Is there something here that grabs your heart? Or what have I not even thought of? Jesus has something significant he wants *you* to do. But I might disappoint you here. And maybe I should. God doesn't need any chest-pounding or swagger or pushiness from us. His surprising strategies are Jesus-like—not impressive, but very effective: "The foolishness of God is wiser than men, and the weakness of God is stronger than men" (1 Cor. 1:25).

Yes, as time goes by, the evils of this present world will get worse. You will see horrible things in your time. But you will also see glorious things. Don't fear the darkness. Spread the light. You're on the winning side. "The light shines in the darkness, and the darkness has not overcome it" (John 1:5).

In fact, the worse things get, the more men will want to join you. They will see in you and your brothers a life-giving alternative. I am praying that, by God's grace, *one million men* will rally to his noble cause.

Here's why I'm so confident. We aren't building the new world. Jesus is building it, and he's giving us the privilege of getting involved.[2] So give him the glory for your every success. But you don't have to make good things happen. *He* will—again and again—until his new world is fully established.

For the earth will be filled
    with the knowledge of the glory of the LORD
    as the waters cover the sea. (Hab. 2:14)

2   I thank Francis Schaeffer (1912–1984) for teaching me this humble confidence.

Your part, in your generation, is just to keep on and keep on and keep on. T. S. Eliot explained how freeing it is to live this way: "For us, there is only the trying. The rest is not our business."[3]

I love that. Here's why. Nobody bats a thousand. But just the trying is itself noble. So keep going, and never quit. And when I'm with the Lord above, I'll be so proud of you, rejoicing at every risk you take for his sake.

Following Jesus always includes risk, even danger—*of course.* "Dangers there must be; how else can you keep a story going?"[4] Your life story will be far more powerful for the hardships you bravely accept. Would you *want* it any other way?

The courage that will help you every day is defined honestly by Atticus Finch in *To Kill a Mockingbird*: "I wanted you to see what real courage is, instead of getting the idea that courage is a man with a gun in his hand. It's when you know you're licked before you begin, but you begin anyway, and you see it through no matter what. You rarely win, but sometimes you do."[5]

How could it be otherwise? Our lives are retelling the story of Jesus. He died, but then he rose again. Which proves he can reverse defeats into victories. Always remember that, Son. The death of porn will never happen by our cunning and threats. That human fraudulence is how the porn industry succeeds! The only way a noble world can replace this predatory world is *the Jesus way*—as you follow him down into death (Phil. 2:1–11). I'm talking about sacrifice, loss, humiliation, steady faithfulness over the years, sticking your neck out, being opposed by powerful people—or even just ignored.

3   T. S. Eliot, "East Coker," in *Four Quartets* (New York: Harcourt, Brace, 1943), stanza 5.
4   C. S. Lewis, "On Stories," in *Of Other Worlds: Essays and Stories*, ed. Walter Hooper (New York: Harcourt, Brace, 1966), 4.
5   Harper Lee, *To Kill A Mockingbird* (New York: Lippincott, 1960), 128.

But those are *the very places* where he will give you experiences of his life-giving resurrection power. Nothing in all this pushy world can defeat your mighty Ally. So I can see you and your brothers reaching out to thousands of men and women, and you're paying a price, and they're discovering their royalty, and you guys will be able to say—gratefully—to them, "We are always facing death, but this means that you know more and more of life" (2 Cor. 4:12 Phillips). What a privilege! It's how even the world of porn can be transformed into a world of nobility. Keep following Jesus down into death and up into resurrection—again and again. It worked for him. It'll work for you. He'll make sure of it.

So when you do lose yardage—even the best teams do sometimes—put your trust in *the One who bounced back from death*, get back up, and keep moving forward. One day will pass into the next, one year will pass into the next, and you'll soon find yourself an old man like me. You'll look around at the vast army of men of integrity who, with you, are building a world of nobility, with *multitudes* of men and women and boys and girls newly alive through Jesus. You will be astonished—and very happy.

But between here and there, *what's your plan?* The Lord will nudge you in the direction he has for you: "God is working in you, giving you the desire and the power to do what pleases him" (Phil. 2:13 NLT). And here are some significant possibilities I don't have the expertise to go into:

- Earn as much money as you lawfully can, and plow tons of it into the cause of liberation. There are heroic anti-porn, anti-trafficking organizations that deserve your financial support. If God has given you the knack for making significant money, use it for human good and his glory. Go fund the liberators!

- Lobby your political leaders at all levels to investigate, expose, regulate, and limit the porn industry, as much as freedom of expression allows. How can our society tolerate revenge porn, rape porn, child porn? All of it is on the web. What else are laws for, if not for diminishing and punishing such brutality? Politics is not the highest form of power, but it is far from nothing. If you are well connected politically, use your influence!

- Educate the rising generation in our history and our stories of nobility. Every generation must learn afresh, at home and in school, how magnificently this life can be lived. If God calls you to be a teacher or a coach or a school principal—and certainly, if you are a father—inspire your children, your students, your athletes with the code of chivalry and knighthood and hero-ism, the stories of courage and virtue and sacrifice, the ideal of a gentleman who puts "women and children first," ahead of himself, and so forth. Those kids won't laugh at you—not if they've seen it in you. And if you *don't* fill their imaginations with greatness, porn *will* fill their minds with ugliness. Our kids long for nobility. God has planted it deep within them. Teach them how to be at their best!

There is so much good you can do. But I'll kick off my own proposals with something *every* man must do.

1. Stay on the Anvil

Here's your biggest contribution to God's new world. Just *be* a man of growing integrity. Who you are deep in your heart empowers what you do out in the public eye.

Your personal goal is nothing less than to be "a vessel for honor-able use, set apart as holy, useful to the master of the house, ready for every good work" (2 Tim. 2:21). As your Master shapes you into that vessel for honorable use, the devil's world of oppression loses ground, more than you can see. The crucial battle is won deep within you. Then you'll be ready for whatever public impact he plans to give you.

Not that it's easy. This old poem tells us, in blunt language, how the Lord hammers on us for his royal purposes:

When God wants to drill a man
And thrill a man
And skill a man
When God wants to mold a man
To play the noblest part

When He yearns with all His heart
To create so great and bold a man
That all the world shall be amazed,
Watch His methods, watch His ways!
How He ruthlessly perfects
Whom He royally elects!

How He hammers him and hurts him
And with mighty blows converts him
Into shapes and forms of clay
Which only God can understand!

How He bends but never breaks
When his good He undertakes
How He uses whom He chooses
And with mighty power infuses him
With every act induces him

To try His splendor out!

God knows what He's about.[6]

Stay there on his anvil, Son, however his hammer falls. It's a hard place. But it won't make *you* hard. It's where God reshapes you for the gentle authority that moves history.

The men who chip away at the porn industry will be the men who've had their own rough edges knocked off.

2. Tell Your Story

Along the way, how are you changing? Where were you before, and where are you now? That story deserves to be told.

Why not compose an "elevator conversation"—as short as the time it takes to ride from, say, the first floor to the fourth? It's a simple narrative of your before-and-after—not how Jesus saved you in the past but how Jesus is helping you in the present. Be ready to share it with anyone at any time. Your story—the more vulnerable, the better—might earn you a longer conversation at another time.

Your experience will give hope to men who are drifting. They feel stuck. They want out. But they can't see an exit sign anywhere in their world. That's where you come in. Tell them *how* you're breaking free. Many men will join you and your brothers. It starts with small talk—which is a big deal.

How about sitting down at your laptop and thinking it through? Your goal is "a good story *well told*."[7] So make your words modest, few, and from the heart. When a friend does you the honor of listening, just tell him, in a forthright, gentle way, how Jesus is

---

6   Adapted by an anonymous author from "When Nature Wants a Man," in *Forward, March!*, by Angela Morgan (New York: John Lane, 1918), 92–95, which is in the public domain.

7   Robert McKee, *Story: Substance, Structure, Style, and the Principles of Screenwriting* (New York: Regan, 1997), 21. Italics original.

surprising you. It is very loving to open a new door for someone else, whether or not he decides to walk through it.

And humor helps. Laughter *can't* be pompous. And surely your story has some hilarity built into it. Capitalize on that. Who expects a *Christian* story to include laughing at ourselves? But it should.

Doesn't everyone need a hope bigger than their own idiot moments? And how can the porn industry thrive in a world where more and more men are talking Jesus up—and enjoying it—rather than dragging women down?

3. Pray

Prayer is a surprising strategy for changing the world. Prayer feels weak. We feel awkward trying. So we neglect prayer.

But our prayers to God are not weak. They are powerful, because God is powerful. And if we feel inept at prayer, that's okay. Here's why: "God fixes our prayers on the way up. If he does not answer the prayer we made, he will answer the prayer we should have made. That is all anyone needs to know."[8]

Should you get together with your brothers and devise smart plans for promoting a world of nobility right where you are? Yes. Plan, execute, evaluate, adjust, get better at it, and keep going. *But we should also pray before, during, and after everything else we do.* Why so much prayer? For two reasons.

First, we're picking a fight with demons: "We do not wrestle against flesh and blood, but against the rulers, against the authorities, against the cosmic powers over this present darkness" (Eph. 6:12). What would you think of soldiers who go up against enemy tanks with squirt guns? That's us—without

8   J. I. Packer and Carolyn Nystrom, *Praying: Finding Our Way through Duty to Delight* (Downers Grove, IL: InterVarsity Press, 2006), 175.

prayer. We're not just fighting websites. We're fighting the unseen forces that put their dazzling, blinding powers on the surface of porn's hideous evils.

In a way, I find the Bible's teaching about Satan comforting. It means that we human beings aren't responsible for *all* the evil in this world. But it's also sobering. It's why Jesus taught us to *pray*, "Deliver us from evil" (Matt. 6:13). Washington can't do that for us. But God can. Only God can.

Which gives us a second reason for saturating every effort with prayer: we're fighting our battles by God's strategies. "The weapons we fight with are not the weapons of the world. On the contrary, they have divine power to demolish strongholds" (2 Cor. 10:4 NIV). We don't have to get mean. We have prayer. The early Christians understood that, and it's why they kept winning—against the odds. For example, the apostle Paul wrote, "Strive together with me in your prayers to God on my behalf" (Rom. 15:30). And this "striving" language means fighting, struggling. It's how we call on God to send in the reinforcements only he commands against powers only he can defeat.

Think of your King this way, and you'll pray more confidently.

The Lord Jesus Christ reigns today. He is in the control room of the universe. All the sins of man and machinations of Satan ultimately have to enhance the glory and kingdom of our Saviour. We have become too enemy-conscious. We need to be more God-conscious, so that we can laugh the laugh of faith, knowing that we have power over all the power of the enemy (Luke 10:19). He has already lost control because of Calvary, where the Lamb was slain.[9]

9 Patrick Johnstone, *Operation World* (Kent: STL, 1987), 21.

So let's pray not just *against* the allure of porn but also *for* the power of the Holy Spirit. Jesus said, "If you then, who are evil, know how to give good gifts to your children, how much more will the heavenly Father give the Holy Spirit to those who ask him!" (Luke 11:13). We think, *The better the gift, the less God is willing to give it.* But the truth is the opposite. "*How much more* will the heavenly Father give the Holy Spirit . . ." We don't have to deserve the Holy Spirit, but we do have to ask: ". . . to those who *ask him*!" God is calling us into lifestyle prayer so that we experience lifelong power.

Real kingdom advance isn't mechanical or automatic, like an assembly line with us pushing buttons and in control. Real kingdom advance is personal—our King himself drawing near to you and your brothers, sensitive to you, listening to you. It's you guys asking him for his power again and again. What he's after is not just a whole new world of nobility but a whole new world of nobility *so obviously miraculous* that you're blown away by what only he can do. Prayer is where that miracle keeps happening.

You can start each day with a simple prayer for yourself. Like this: "Lord, I needed you yesterday. I need you again today. You've given me a task that's beyond me. So please give me more of the Holy Spirit right now, however you see my need. Thank you. In your holy name. Amen." It isn't complicated. It's just the Lord's Prayer—"Your kingdom come"—in your own words. It will work, not because you're twisting God's arm but precisely because you don't have to twist his arm. Not because your words are convincing but because your Father is willing.

You can pray also for worldwide awakening. Wouldn't it be amazing to see the next historic revival starting deep inside the porn industry? I have no time for "revival" if all it means is some nice suburban church improving its comfortable lifestyle while easing into heaven on cruise control. The revival I'm praying for is the risen King coming down into the lowest hell of porn and gently forgiving the bosses, the investors, the videographers, the performers, the website managers, the advertisers, the users, and everyone driving that engine of oppression. Our King can pour out upon anyone a joy they've *never* known. And I will never stop praying for that. Will you join me?

If we ask for that mighty blessing, I'll be *shocked* if Jesus says no.

4. Get Married

Unless Jesus calls you to serve him as a single man, get married! And love your wife well! Marriage is an underrated strategy for changing the world.

And don't wait until you find the perfect soul mate, until your career goals are fulfilled, and until you can afford a comfortable life together. Real love isn't that calculating. For crying out loud, Son, it's easier than all that. Just fall crazy-in-love with a woman in love with Jesus, and get married! Your marriage will be both imperfect and miraculous. The Lord will be with you and your wife just as much as he was with Adam and Eve.

Marriage is prophetic. A healthy marriage, earthy as it is, makes the love of Christ more visible and believable to a skeptical world. *You* don't have to be amazing. Marriage *itself* is amazing—two sinners giving grace and receiving grace "as long as they both shall live." Who could deny the beauty of that?

And if your wife was mistreated in this world of brutality, she'll bring that suffering into your marriage. It means the Lord is giving you a sacred privilege. You can prove to *her* that his love is real.

My dear wife, Jani, asked if it might be helpful to include her story at this point. Naturally, I'm honored for her to speak.

I grew up in a home where my dad did not love my mom—or me—well. For many years he guarded his heart *from* Christ, rather than bringing his heart *to* Christ. A deep pain from my childhood is that he molested me for some years, until I was old enough to say, "If you do this again, I'll tell Mom." So he finally left me alone. I've always regretted not going to someone for help. But I didn't have the words or the maturity to get past my own nauseating confusion and humiliation.

When I met Ray—my hero in every way—again I didn't have the wisdom or courage to tell him about this dark place in my younger years. Much of it was hidden deep in suppressed memories. But eventually it all started resurfacing. I knew I had to talk it through with my beloved husband. How would he respond?

Ray could have felt betrayed or angry or repulsed. He could have withdrawn. Instead, he drew me in, closer than ever. He told me: "Darling, this doesn't change us. It only makes me want to love you more tenderly and protect you more fiercely. I have always and only felt privileged to be your husband. Please let me love you." The love of Jesus himself gently washed over me.

God has used Ray to redeem my past. He has blessed us with a deeply satisfying marriage. He gave me the privilege of marrying a man who has loved me well.

Jesus creates win-win marriages in a lose-lose world. If your wife's heart was broken, you can build a new world of nobility right there at home. Love her with gentle understanding. God gave her to you so that she can experience his love through your love. She deserves it.

Your home address is where your family, and many friends who visit, can experience the healing presence of the King *with generational impact*.

5. Create

Music means a lot to me as a Nashville pastor. It's powerful for building a new world of nobility. Here's why. Andrew Fletcher, a Scottish politician long ago, wisely said, "If a man were permitted to make all the ballads, he need not care who should make the laws of a nation."[10] Of course. Music shapes us more than laws do. Music moves our hearts. Which is why singing together is a creative force for a whole new world.

I remember the civil rights movement of the 1960s, with Bob Dylan and Mahalia Jackson and others giving the people music that validated their longings and inspired their courage. Here's a true story from that era.

Jamila Jones, as a girl in 1958, went to the Highlander Folk School in Tennessee for training in activism. The police raided her school. The city shut off the electrical power. In the darkness of that night Jamila and her young friends began to sing "We are not afraid" to the tune of "We Shall Overcome." In an interview recorded by the Library of Congress, Jamila told us what happened next:

> We got louder and louder with singing that verse, until one of the policemen came and he said to me, "If you have to sing," and he was actually shaking, "do you have to sing so loud?" And I could not believe it. Here these people had all the guns, the billy clubs, the power, we thought. And he was asking me, with a shake, if I would not sing so loud. And it was that time that I really understood the power of our music.[11]

---

10 *The Political Works of Andrew Fletcher* (London, 1732), 372. I thank my friend Tom Douglas, the Nashville songwriter, for helping me find this quotation. Fletcher went on to say that most lawmakers of the past found they could not reform a nation without the help of a song.

11 "Music in the Civil Rights Movement," Library of Congress, https://www.loc.gov/collections/civil-rights-history-project/articles-and-essays/music-in-the-civil-rights-movement/.

Who has written the "We Shall Overcome" of our generation? Where are the musicians—plus the novelists, painters, film-makers, photographers, poets, sculptors, and others—who are giving us songs and images and stories for lament, for protest, for confidence and courage and joy and sacrifice and victory? How many churches today have in their repertoire songs and liturgies and readings for our fight *against* the degradation of porn and *for* the nobility of justice, the way nineteenth-century churches had the abolitionist "Battle Hymn of the Republic" as their rallying cry? *Why is it even hard for us to imagine a church singing that way today?* What a blind spot! We've got some catch-up work to do!

Is our Lord calling you to fight for nobility with the powerful weapons of art?

6. Advocate

There is a way for any man, in any calling, to advocate for a new world of nobility. And it's more powerful than politics.[12]

God's way is so simple, it's downright unimpressive—but also doable. Just go public as a man experiencing healing from God. It's a brave step to take. Of course, if you're married, talk it through with your wife ahead of time. (Always respect her feelings.) And be wise in what you say and where you say it. But especially with your brothers in confession and prayer and healing—what I described in my last letter—the more open and vulnerable you become, the more men will join you. And small personal changes will grow, over time, into big social changes. *Brotherhood can replace porn more powerfully than laws can ban porn.*

---

12 I thank my friend, Dr. Russell Moore of the Ethics and Religious Liberty Commission, for suggesting to me, in personal conversation, this line of reasoning.

Your brotherhood is public proof of the new world of nobility, where men can see that "God is really among you" (1 Cor. 14:25). His surprisingly gentle grace will deeply resonate as more men become aware of what's possible, thanks to him.

Many guys have given up. They "budget" for porn in their consciences. They can't even imagine life without it—until they *see* men who are getting free.

The Fantasyland of porn inevitably becomes a living hell. Then a man might start looking for an exit, the same way you did. But this time, you'll be there for him. Make the brotherhood option publicly obvious, easy to find. That's powerful advocacy!

Again—the more approachable you are, the more compelling. It's hard to let other men know where you've been and what you've done. But soldiers of the King do hard things, for his sake: "Share in suffering as a good soldier of Christ Jesus" (2 Tim. 2:3).

Oh, and this too. The technology that spreads porn can also grow brotherhood. Don't just play defense. Go on offense. Go blast open the gates of hell (Matt. 16:18)! Build a website with videos and stories and images of what healthy brotherhood can look like. Keep it real. No misleading "success stories." But lots of honesty, and lots of laughter.

Advocate publicly for the King's new world of nobility as an alternative so obviously encouraging that any man would *love* to jump in!

7. Rejoice

Yes, you read that right. *Rejoice.* Does it seem a small thing? It isn't. Joy is powerful. Joy from on high makes you and your brothers a wave of renewal for an exhausted generation.

Don't get me wrong. It is *not* a sin to be sad about sad things. Jesus said, "Blessed are those who mourn" (Matt. 5:4). But it *is* a sin to be ungrateful, touchy, grumpy. Like when a man puts his foot down and says: "This rotten life you've given me, God—*really?* This is the best you've got?" Turning to porn is easy then. It isn't about sex. It's about self-pity. It's one sin spiraling down to an even deeper sin. How can that end well?

But here is what Satan fears: men of God, like us, rejoicing our fool heads off! He doesn't fear our brilliance. He's more brilliant. He doesn't even fear our good behavior. He can twist morality into hypocrisy. What Satan fears is a man shattered, stripped of his dreams, so devastated that all he has left is Jesus—and to Jesus that man turns. In his anguish, his trauma, that man falls at the feet of Jesus with nothing but desperate need. And *to that man* the risen King speaks, as only he can, saying, "I will never leave you nor forsake you" (Heb. 13:5). And that man weeps—*for joy.* That broken man is the mighty warrior Satan fears.

Satan's scam, the porn industry, stands to lose big-time the more you and your brothers experience the industrial-strength joy of the Lord. The greatest power for good in all the world doesn't require a committee motion and a majority vote. It's simple: your joy in Christ. Not your iron will but your rejoicing heart. The word will get out, and more men will join you.

The Bible commands us, "Rejoice in the Lord always; again I will say, rejoice" (Phil. 4:4). But don't read that to mean, "Always be chipper, upbeat, peppy." No, "Rejoice *in the Lord*" means this: however crazy things get, *as long as the Lord is the Lord,* we will always have a reason to rejoice. If we obsess on the question *Why is this hardship happening to me?* we'll never rejoice. But if we'll keep asking, *What is it about* the Lord *that can help me in my need right now?* we'll be surprised by all we find—and all we feel.

For example—worst-case scenario—you're closing your laptop after giving in yet again. It doesn't take long to start feeling defeat, disgust, shame. But what is *the Lord* feeling about you right at that moment? "My compassion grows warm and tender" (Hos. 11:8). "My heart yearns for him" (Jer. 31:20). Your King is "a friend of . . . sinners" (Matt. 11:19), not their enemy. When you sin, he is your "advocate" (1 John 2:1), not your accuser. Taking his stand as your Helper and Ally is his holy calling—his job, you might say. And he *loves* his job. He is joyously committed to your joyous integrity. It's what he honestly feels about you, simply because that's who he is, way down deep, now and forever. So go ahead and rejoice in the Lord right now, as you are, defying your own ridiculousness.

Want to give Satan a bad day? Rejoice in the Lord. Want to strengthen your brothers? Rejoice in the Lord. Want to stay steady through temptation? Rejoice in the Lord. Want to expose the emptiness of porn? Rejoice in the Lord. Want to empower the cause of justice? Rejoice in the Lord. Joy is the greatest power in the universe. No wonder the Bible says, "Rejoice in the Lord always."

Here is my final appeal, Son. Will you commit *right now* to rejoicing in the Lord, all your days, as your determined mindset? You can be this decisive:

> I will praise the LORD as long as I live;
> > I will sing praises to my God while I have my being.
> > > (Ps. 146:2)

Here's what that resolve can look like. True story.

My dad was a pastor. One day he got a phone call from out of the blue. A family visiting our city found "Rev. Ray Ortlund" in the phone book and dialed his number. Their elderly father was suddenly dying, and they needed a pastor. So Dad jumped in the car and drove down to the hospital. Dad stood there at the bedside of this elderly gentleman, reading Scripture and praying. Then he noticed that the dying man's lips were moving. So Dad leaned over to hear what he was saying. After all, last words are lasting words! What was this old man whispering with his final breaths? "Praise the Lord! Praise the Lord! Praise the Lord!" It was the joy of Psalm 146:2 in real life—and death. Dad never forgot it. He passed it on to me. Now I pass it on to you.

Very soon you will be that old man. You will be on your death-bed. You might have the strength for only a few final words. Can you imagine gasping out, "Oh, precious porn, thank you, thank you, thank you!"?

Son, you can die *magnificently*. You can whisper, with your final breath: "Praise the Lord! Praise the Lord! Praise the Lord!" Hell will shudder with screams of demonic pain to lose you so finally. Heaven will shout with raucous angelic joy to receive you so eternally. And you will leave behind a better world.

Well done!

Because you'll never regret it,
Ray

Acknowledgments

LIFE IS A GROUP PROJECT, and I enjoy that. I am especially grateful for all who helped me with this particular project.

First and foremost, my wife, Jani, prayed me through this. I needed it. She also read and critiqued the manuscript and, courageously, added her own story to letter 6.

My agents, Robert and Andrew Wolgemuth, joined me in daring to believe that a whole generation of men are ready to experience their true nobility. I am grateful for their personal solidarity.

My editors, Lawrence Kimbrough and Thom Notaro, wrapped their brilliant minds around the book as a whole and offered many insightful suggestions for sharpening my prose.

Other friends reviewed the manuscript, to various degrees, enriching my argument with their own insights and experiences: Jennifer Cortez, Jarrett DeLozier, Nancy French, Gary McDonald, Gavin Ortlund, Barnabas Piper, Derri Smith, and my brave friend Tara.

My friend Thabiti Anyabwile, whom I highly respect, contributed the foreword, for which I thank him.

Still more friends contributed in other ways: Sam Allberry, Brian Bobel, Jason Cheek, Tom Douglas, Chris Hickman, Russell Moore, Dane and Stacey Ortlund, Eric and Erin Ortlund, Esther Ortlund,

John and Krista Scheidt, Bruce Waltke, Jessica Waterman, Darryl Williamson, and John Woodbridge.

Finally, I thank the board and supporters of Renewal Ministries, the elders and pastors of Immanuel Church, and everyone at Crossway for their support and prayers. And I will always owe a debt of gratitude to the men of Immanuel Church for all those Tuesday evenings through the years—at Immanuel Theology for Men—where we learned how to be honest (1 John 1:7) and how to honor one another (Rom. 12:10). Until I experienced it with you guys, I would not have believed it.

"To him who loves us and has freed us from our sins by his blood and made us a kingdom, priests to his God and Father, to him be glory and dominion forever and ever. Amen" (Rev. 1:5–6).

Appendix

A Man's Identity

David Powlison

WHO ARE YOU? What gives a man his identity? On what foundation are you building your sense of self? Your answer, whether true
or false, defines your life.[1]

Wrong ways of defining who we are arise naturally in our hearts,
and the world around us preaches and models innumerable false
identities. But Jesus maps out and walks out a counterintuitive and
countercultural way to know who you are. Your true identity is a
gift of God, a surprising discovery, and then a committed choice.

What are the ways men get identity wrong? Perhaps you con-
struct a self by the roles and accomplishments listed on your ré-
sumé. You might identify yourself by your lineage or ethnicity,
by your job history or the schools you attended, by your marital
status or parental role. Perhaps you define who you are by your
political leanings or the objects of your sexual longings. Maybe
you consider yourself to be summed up in a Myers-Briggs category

1 From the *ESV Men's Devotional Bible* (Wheaton, IL: Crossway, 2015), 1533–35.

or a psychiatric diagnosis. Your sense of self might be based on money (or your lack thereof), on achievements (or failures), on the approval of others (or their rejection), on your self-esteem (or self-hatred). Perhaps you think that your sins define you: an angry man, an addict, an anxious people-pleaser. Perhaps afflictions define you: disability, cancer, divorce. Even your Christian identity might anchor in something that is not God: Bible knowledge, giftedness, or the church denomination to which you belong.

In each case, your sense of identity comes unglued from the God who actually defines you.

God's way of sizing up a man goes against the grain of our instinctive opinions and strategies. Here are six basic realities to orient you:

- Your true identity is who God says you are. You will never discover who you are by looking inside yourself or listening to what others say. The Lord gets the *first* word because he made you. He gets the *daily* word because you live before his face. He gets the *last* word because he will administer your "comprehensive life review."
- Your true identity inseparably connects you to God. Everything you ever learn about who God is—*his* identity—correlates specifically to something about who you are. For example, "your Father knows your need" means you are always a dependent child. "Jesus Christ is your Lord" means you are always a servant.
- Who God is also correlates with how you express your core identity as your various roles in life develop. For example, the Bible says that God's compassion for you is like that of a father with his children (Ps. 103:13). You will always be a dependent child at your core, but as you grow up into God's image, you become increasingly able to care for others in a fatherly way.

- Your instinctive sense of identity is skewed. In the act of suppressing the knowledge of God (Rom. 1:18–23), a fallen heart suppresses true self-knowing. Whenever we forget God, we forget who we are.
- A true and enduring identity is a complex gift of Christ's grace. He gives a new identity in an act of mercy. Then his Spirit makes it a living reality over a lifetime. When you see him face to face, you will know him as he truly is, and you will fully know who you are (1 Cor. 13:12).
- Your new and true identity connects you to God's other children in a common calling. It is not individualistic. You are one member in the living body of Christ.

Now consider a few of the details. Don't skim through. You will never be gripped by these truths if you treat them merely as an information download.

- All good gifts, beginning with life itself, come from God. You will never be independent. The Lord sustains our lives physically. And every word from the mouth of God gives life. And, supremely, Jesus Christ is the bread of life. Faith knows and embraces this core identity: "I am his *dependent*."
- Our dependency as created beings is compounded, complicated, and intensified by sins and by sufferings. To know ourselves truly is to know our need for help. Faith knows and embraces this core identity: "I am *poor* and *weak*."
- The Lord is merciful to the wayward. He redeems the sinful, forgetful, and blind. Faith knows and embraces this core identity: "I am *sinful*—but I am *forgiven*."
- God is our Father. He adopts us in Christ, and by the power of the Spirit, he gives us a childlike heart. We need parenting every

day. We need tender care, patient instruction, and constructive discipline. Faith knows and embraces this core identity: "I am God's *child*."

- The Lord is our refuge. Our lives are beset by a variety of troubles, threats, and disappointments. We aren't strong enough to stand up to what we face. God's presence is the only safe place. Faith knows and embraces this core identity: "I am a *refugee*."
- The Lord is our shepherd. He laid down his life for the sheep. He watches over our going out and coming in. We need looking after and continual oversight. Faith knows and embraces this core identity: "I am a *sheep* in his flock."
- Christ is Lord and Master. He bought us with a price; we belong to him. We need someone to tell us what to do and how to do it. Faith knows and embraces this core identity: "I am a *servant*, indentured for life."
- The Lord is married to his people. He patiently nourishes and cherishes his wife, the living body of Christ. We need husbanding from someone faithful, kind, protective, and generous. Faith knows and embraces this core identity: "I *submit* to Jesus."
- God searches every man's heart. We live before his eyes. Faith knows and embraces this core identity: "I am a *God-fearing* man."
- Our God is good, mighty, and glorious. He is worthy of our trust, esteem, gladness, and gratitude. Faith knows and embraces this core identity: "I am a *worshiper*."

We could go on! The pattern is obvious. Every core aspect of a man's identity expresses some form of humility, need, submission, and dependency before the Lord. Our culture and our hearts might claim that masculinity means being independent, self-confident, proud, strong, assertive, decisive, tough-minded, opinionated, and unemotional. But Jesus is the true man, and he is unafraid of weakness, lowliness, and submission. He came as a helpless and endangered child. He became dependent, poor, afflicted, homeless, submitted—an obedient servant entrusted with a job to do. He became a mere man and died in pain—committing his spirit into God's hands, depending by faith on the power of the Spirit to raise him. He feels every emotion expressed in the Psalms.

Yet Jesus is also strong. He is leader, teacher, and Lord. He speaks with decisive authority. He helps the weak. He forgives the sinful. He has mercies to give away. He faces the hostility of men with courage and clarity. He lives purposefully. He goes out looking for his lost sheep. He does the things God does.

How did these two things fit together in Jesus' life, and how do they fit together in ours? Here is the pattern: Core identity as a man leads to the calling to act like God. Weakness leads to strength. Serving leads to mastery. Deaths lead to resurrections. It never works the other way around. When your core identity is meek and lowly—like Jesus—then your calling develops into his image of purposeful, wise, courageous love. You become like God.

The order matters. You become generous and merciful to others by continually receiving generous mercies. You learn how to protect others by finding refuge in the Lord. You develop into a good father by living as a well-fathered child of your Father. You develop into a masterful leader by living as a well-mastered servant. You develop into a wise teacher by being a well-taught learner. You learn how to husband a wife in love by being well-husbanded by Christ. You develop into a caring pastor of others by living as a well-pastored sheep of your Shepherd. You become a surprisingly good counselor by being well-counseled by your Wonderful Counselor.

Of course, in much of life, we function in roles where others are over us, and we live in honorable dependency and submission. "Be subject for the Lord's sake to every human institution" (1 Pet.

2:13). Leaders in one sphere submit in other spheres. The pastor of your church is subject to the church's governing authorities. A father of children owes honor to his own mother and father. When your core identity is in Christ, you bear fruit whether he calls you to serve as a leader or to serve as a servant.

Finally, consider that all your present callings will someday come to an end. When you grow old, frail, and helpless, you will become someone else's charge and responsibility. But your true identity is imperishable. You will still abide in Christ. And when he appears, you will appear with him in glory (Col. 3:4).

General Index

Scripture Index

Other Crossway Books by Ray Ortlund

The Gospel: How the Church Portrays the Beauty of Christ

Isaiah: God Saves Sinners

Marriage and the Mystery of the Gospel

Proverbs: Wisdom That Works